MINISTERS OF THE KINGDOM

MINISTERS OF THE KINGDOM

Exploration in Non-Stipendiary Ministry

edited by
PETER BAELZ & WILLIAM JACOB

CIO PUBLISHING
Church House, Dean's Yard, London SW1P 3NZ

ISBN 0 7151 2541 9

Published 1985 for the Advisory Council for the Church's Ministry
by CIO Publishing

Printed and bound in Great Britain by Burgess & Son (Abingdon) Ltd.

CONTENTS

THE CONTRIBUTORS

Peter Baelz is Dean of Durham and Chairman of the ACCM Committee for Theological Education

Robin Bennett is Archdeacon of Dudley

Anthony Birbeck is a Management Consultant with the Coverdale Organisation

Ian Cundy is Warden of Cranmer Hall, Durham

Mike Hatt is a local authority engineer with Devon County Council

William Jacob is Secretary of the ACCM Committee for Theological Education

Robert Langley is Principal of St Albans Ministerial Training Scheme and a Residentiary Canon of St Albans

James Mark was until recently an editor of *Theology*

Kenneth Noakes is Rector of Marhamchurch, Cornwall

Alan Payne is Rector of St Thomas's, Stanningley, Leeds

Martin Thornton is a Canon Residentiary and Chancellor of Truro Cathedral

Patrick Vaughan is Principal of the East Midlands Ministry Training Course

FOREWORD

In 1983 ACCM published the report of a research project, *Non-Stipendiary Ministry in the Church of England,* by Dr Mark Hodge. That report was a factual account of developments in non-stipendiary ministry during the preceding fifteen years or so. When the ACCM Council received Dr Hodge's report the need was noted for some discussion about the place of non-stipendiary ministry in the theology of the Church and its ministry, and the Dean of Durham, as Chairman of the Committee for Theological Education, was invited to consider how such a discussion might be promoted.

The Dean, in consultation with Dr Jacob, the Secretary of the Committee for Theological Education, invited a number of people to contribute essays on various theological implications of non-stipendiary ministry. Having been edited, these have now been received by the Council, who wish to commend them for study by all who are concerned about or involved in this development in the Church's ministry. The Council are glad to make this symposium available as a companion volume to Dr Hodge's research in the hope that together they will inform and stimulate a debate throughout the Church, more particularly in the General Synod, about the best means of furthering this ministry.

The Council wishes to place on record its thanks to the Dean of Durham and Dr Jacob for undertaking the task of collecting and editing the essays and to all those who have contributed essays for this collection.

ALEC NEWCASTLE
Chairman of the
Advisory Council for
the Church's Ministry

INTRODUCTION

When the idea of a research project on non-stipendiary ministry was first conceived it was intended that a section of the report should be devoted to theological reflections. It was subsequently recognised, however, that such a section would differ in kind from the rest of Dr Hodge's report and the Council of ACCM therefore invited the Dean of Durham, as Chairman of their Committee for Theological Education, to consider how best to promote a discussion about the place of non-stipendiary ministry in the theology of the Church.

Several distinct but related questions needed to be tackled, for example to what extent is the parochial model of ministry primary? Is it possible to be a 'priest' without being a 'clergyman'? What are the essential functions of priesthood and what is the point of ordination? Is it possible or useful to distinguish between historical, sociological, ecclesiastical and theological points of view? Can experience and practice illuminate our theological and theoretical understanding? Can work itself be a form of ministry? It seemed that the best means of promoting a discussion of these questions was to invite a number of people, including those who had had direct experience of non-stipendiary ministry, to contribute to a collection of essays on these issues.

When the essays were received it became apparent that the task of producing a reasonably compact and coherent work would not be easy. The essays varied a lot in length and style. Clearly there would have to be considerable editing in order to provide connecting links between them. Some of the material, though valuable in its own right, would have to be sacrificed because the topics suggested had turned out to be peripheral to the central concern. There was a problem of repetition between the essays. Some repetition was inevitable and would not matter; but too much would detract from the impact it was hoped the essays might have.

Some of the essays in the resulting collection appear more or less in their original form, others have been slightly modified. Sadly, however, the editors felt it necessary to omit several essays, although quotations from all of them have been included where they touch on important matters not mentioned elsewhere. The essays which were omitted because they were somewhat apart from the central concern were those written by James Mark on the work of Readers, by Alan Christmas from the perspective of an industrial chaplain, by Tony Williamson on the experience of being a worker priest, and Tony Birbeck and Alan Payne on the experience of transferring from stipendiary to non-stipendiary ministry and vice versa. We hope they will accept our apologies and are grateful to them for allowing us to use their work in such a cavalier fashion. We regret that as the shape of the collection emerged it became clear that we had been over-ambitious in our original plan.

We should like to thank everyone who responded so willingly to our invitation to contribute. Another occasion might have produced a larger and more representative volume.

I THEOLOGICAL PERSPECTIVE

Non-stipendiary ministers come in various shapes and sizes. What they have in common is the negative characteristic that they are not being paid for the ministry they undertake. They are 'amateurs' rather than 'professionals'. However, the nature of their ministry differs from person to person and from place to place. For example, a recent report identifies five headings under which non-stipendiary ministry is at present exercised: (1) a parish-focused ministry, exercised by a person in full-time secular employment; (2) a parish-focused ministry, exercised by a person who is not in, or who has retired from, secular employment; (3) a work-focused ministry, pastoral and/or prophetic, exercised in the context of a person's secular employment; (4) a 'sector' ministry, in which a person may be exercising a specialist ministry requiring special skills; (5) a 'local' ministry, exercised by a person called by a local community and given the necessary training and authority to minister to that community.[1]

Non-stipendiary ministry, it seems, has been developing under the pressure of circumstances, most obvious among which is the decline in the number of stipendiary ministers. Such a development calls for careful appraisal. Our response to the pressure of circumstances ought not to be blind and unreflecting, nor even purely pragmatic and utilitarian.

A number of searching questions have been raised about non-stipendiary ministry. For example, is the ordained ministry fundamentally compatible with secular employment? If so, is it compatible with all or only with some sorts of employment? How does the ministry of the ordained person in his work-place differ from that which might be expected of any baptized and believing Christian? What difference does ordination make to a person's understanding of himself and his vocation? Is there such a creature as a 'part-time' minister, or are all ordained ministers 'full-time' in virtue of their ordination? Can one be an ordained minister now but not then, or even here but not there – what about the 'catholicity' of orders? Can there be more than one 'kind' of ordained minister? If not, what is it

1

about the ordained minister, the person he is and the work he does, that gives him his special character?

These and other similar questions are *theological* questions. They concern the self-understanding of the Church under the providence of God. Any serious attempt to explore these questions theologically must do justice both to the tradition by which the Church has been shaped, especially the witness of the Scriptures, and also to the actualities of the present situation. Past and present both have a contribution to make to a Christian discernment of the mind of God. We shall expect to find an essential unity in the idea of ministry, if for no other reason than that all ministry derives from the one ministry of Jesus Christ. At the same time we shall expect to find a rich diversity in the expression of that ministry to match the needs of changing circumstances. Unity-in-diversity is a mark of the living Church, and it should not be surprising if it were found to be a mark of the Church's ministry also.

Two theological approaches consequently suggest themselves, although in fact neither can afford to ignore the other. First, there is the approach which attempts to distil from the Scriptures and the traditions of the Church some single, unifying 'idea', or essence, of ministry. The underlying assumption of this approach is that, once this 'idea' has been determined, it may be applied as a pattern to present-day developments, allowing some while forbidding others. Such an approach pays close attention to the *unity* of ministry, but it runs the risk of making that unity too formal and forgetting that the unity of the Spirit may itself create a diversity of forms. Secondly, there is the approach which, without denying the importance of reflection on the biblical and ecclesiastical sources, but anxious that they should not act as a barrier to new insights and new understanding, begins with the existing situation and the developments in ministry which are taking place and asks what needs they are meeting and what lessons they have to teach us about the potential expressions of ministry. According to this approach the 'idea' of ministry is dynamic, clothing itself differently in different situations. It cannot be captured in an unchanging formula; it belongs to the realm of the Spirit. The strength of this approach lies in its openness and exploration; its weakness in its tendency to forget that the present has a history and to mistake passing fashion for eternal truth. There is more than one kind of spirit, and criteria are needed for their testing.

Theological reflection, then, should be dialectical, moving

backwards and forwards between the present and the past, alert to new ways in which the Spirit may be seeking to give expression to the continuing ministry of Jesus Christ. That ministry has a certain unifying character; but just as the character of a human being may express itself in changing circumstances in new and unexpected, but at the same time consistent and continuous, ways, so may the ministry of Jesus Christ as reflected in the ministry of his Church be both creative and coherent. In and through the given structures we must seek the unity of the Spirit. For example, it may be agreed that the threefold ministry which developed in the early Church gave structural expression to a threefold character of Christ's own ministry, namely, his authority, his communication in word and deed, and his service. We may then ask whether this same spirit of authority, communication and service is in fact the essential characteristic of all Christian ministry, wherever and however it is exercised. We may in this way come nearer to answering the question often raised of those who believe they are called to exercise an ordained ministry in and through their secular work, 'What is the point of ordination?'

In the following chapters we shall be looking at some traditional themes of ministry, such as the ministry of the whole people of God and the ordained ministry, calling (vocation) and community, the ministry of word and sacrament, the ministry of prayer, and so on. At the same time we shall be setting these traditional themes in the context of contemporary non-stipendiary ministry, hoping that thereby theme and context may be mutually illuminated. We shall not presume to offer 'definitive' answers to the many theological questions which the development of non-stipendiary ministry is raising. We shall be content if we can see more clearly, and help others to see more clearly, what these questions really are and what kind of 'answers' they might be given out of the Church's living tradition.

We begin with a closer look at the context.

---

[1] *Non-Stipendiary Ministry in the Church of England*, GS 583.

II NON-STIPENDIARY MINISTRY IN CONTEXT

The development of non-stipendiary ministry in this country needs to be set within the widest possible social and ecclesiastical context. Both inside and outside the Church, perceptions, attitudes and expectations have been changing. For example, public life has become more and more secularised, while religion has generally been withdrawing into the sphere of the private, thus leading to an increasingly tenuous relationship between Church and society. At the same time, within the Church itself there has been a deepening sense of being the body of Christ, in which every member has some part or other to play in the Church's mission and ministry. Whether NSM is one more expression of this uncertainty and change, or whether it represents a creative and coherent response to the challenge of change, is one of the fundamental questions on which theological reflection, it is to be hoped, will throw light.

In this chapter Robert Langley ranges widely over the contemporary scene in an attempt to formulate the right questions and to suggest ways in which the Church's thinking and practice might be deepened and strengthened.

Recent years have seen in many parts of the Church of England a mushrooming of a whole variety of authorised but unpaid ministries. The development of non-stipendiary ordained ministry has been part of this wider process, which has not been something inspired from above by the Church as an institution, but represents the response of people who have felt called to offer themselves for further training, work and witness. Behind all of it, I think, lies a suspicion that the present pattern of ministry will not do in today's world. This is perhaps especially true in the case of those who feel themselves called to ordained ministry at work. No doubt their actual explanation of how they see ordained ministry at work is incoherent and open to many questions, but I simply want to affirm the fact that this is just one manifestation of a more general feeling among Christians that all is not well and that new models of relating to our complex society have to be found.

4

That sense of all not being well with the Church's ministry is expressed by Anthony Russell as not just a temporary uncertainty but a profound crisis.[1] This crisis results not only from a feeling of the inadequacy of the matching of patterns of ministry with the needs of society, but also from a deep internal uncertainty about where the Church may look for authority for those forms which it possesses. When Schillebeeckx says that 'the constant in the Church's ministry is always to be found only in specific historically changing forms',[2] and when Richard Hanson judges that, while all denominations have been long accustomed to reading their own structures of ministry into the earliest period of Christianity, yet every such claim must now be disallowed,[3] our insecurity is deep indeed. It is no longer a matter of arguing about which authority in the past is the right one, but whether there is any kind of authority to which we can any longer appeal. The crisis thus exists in two directions at once. Any theology of ministry needs to take its full depth and severity seriously.

Just as I want to suggest that the rise of non-stipendiary ministry is a response to this sense of crisis, so I believe that any discussion of it theologically must be done in the context of the wider questions of the mission and ministry of the Church as a whole. In one sense there can only be theologies of ministry which may include, as one of their constituent parts, rationales for non-stipendiary ministry. Any theology of non-stipendiary ministry is bound to be a function of a theology of ministry as a whole and one strand in the total pattern.

The failure to start from a theology of ministry in thinking about non-stipendiary ministry has often led in the past to three problems. First, the title NSM has come to encompass a wide range of different ministries so that it is no longer possible to be sure what we are talking about. What seems to be happening is the development of a whole variety of different ministerial tasks, some of them traditional, some innovative, some being undertaken without payment, all of them carrying their own assumptions about ministry and the nature of the Church. In this situation the label non-stipendiary really describes what it says and not the nature of the ministerial task. Yet the temptation is to assume that it is a clearly defined category. This leads on to the second problem, since it is because of our tendency to make this assumption and to use this category as a starting point for our theological reflection that we have got into more difficulties. For such an approach leads us easily to assume that the differences in understanding of ordination and priesthood, and the relationship of

5

the Church to the world, which exist in the Church at large, do not somehow come into this discussion. But these issues, discussion of which really does need to be carried on separately, are inevitably sucked in, and our attempts to fashion a theology of non-stipendiary ministry get lost in a fog of ever-larger questions. Thirdly, because NSM is perceived by many primarily as a phenomenon which has grown rather cuckoo-like in the nest of the Church of England, without any clear parenthood, there has been the temptation to try to explain it in terms of understandings and categories derived from the parent we know. In this way the phenomenon is accommodated and prevented from posing too many questions back to the Church as a whole.

Thus we need to start with the mission of the Church in society and then to be clear about what varieties of non-stipendiary ministry we are talking about. The first task is obviously a very large one and there are many different views about it. Different models of the Church will give rise to different understandings of ministry. Any one model will comprehend some of the varieties of non-stipendiary ministry but may well have no place for others.

All I want to try to do is, first, to look at three areas in the general ferment to which I have drawn attention and which I believe are of significance in thinking about non-stipendiary ministry; second, to see if there are any guidelines we can draw from this discussion for the development of a theology of ministry; and third, to focus more specifically on non-stipendiary work-focused ordained ministry.

CHURCH AND SOCIETY

The issues of the Church and the Bomb and the appointment of Bishops reflect nationally a much more widespread concern. At one level this manifests itself in questions about indiscriminate baptism, the disproportionate amount of time demanded in some parishes by the taking of weddings and funerals, and the conduct of civic services. But at a deeper level there is a consciousness that the fit which once existed between the Church and the structures and institutions of society does so no longer in quite the same way.

At a recent meeting to try to discuss a future strategy for a diocese, the matter suddenly became much greater and more profound than one of simply juggling with priorities for diocesan resources, when someone asked the question, what is the diocese? Is it the ecclesiastical organisation of 300 parishes? Is it the county? Or could it be

6

represented only by overlaying a series of maps on the geographical area, showing concentration of population, distribution of industry, communications and movement of people, interaction and dependency on other geographical areas? The parish system in an agricultural society allowed the Church through the vicar to meet people as a matter of course in the whole of their lives. The different maps which it is now possible to draw illustrate powerfully the number of different communities to which most people now belong, and the way in which the forces which shape people's lives are at many levels and usually at a distance from where they live. The parish system is equipped neither by virtue of its geographical rootedness nor by its style of operation to cope on its own with the task of serving society.

If drawing attention to this major shift is one way of describing the process of secularisation, it is also important to point to a continuity of human religious consciousness. Thus, in spite of the pushing of the Church to the periphery of human affairs or to the position of one interest group amongst others, the Church on occasions like baptism still provides people with important symbols. Some would want to stress that the Church's primary task is to 'manage the dependent aspects of corporate life in order to free the community as a whole to cope with other aspects of human existence. . . . In the world of politics and economics, the church is small-time and amateur, but in leading worship and coping with the crisis transitions of life the church possesses the highest level of competence and skill.'[4] Likewise the clergy have symbolic roles; they occupy a boundary between ordinary life and that area where chaos threatens.[5]

While I do not go along with the model of the Church which people like Bruce Reed derive from this kind of analysis, nevertheless I think that the analysis itself is important. It indicates another aspect of the material with which we are dealing, and reminds us of the impossibility of cutting ourselves off from the kinds of roles which historically the clergy and institutional Church have fulfilled, and which sociologically will be laid upon those who claim some religious status in society.

The one thing which most approaches to this question agree on is the importance of lay people. For it is they who are in the front line of our society in a way in which clergy are no longer. The development of non-stipendiary ministry, especially the work-focused variety, is an attempt to create a bridge between society and Church, consciously

7

representing the Church in the secular world and feeding back into the Church the theological insights drawn from their particular experiences. Only in this way, many NSMs believe, can our post-Christian situation be taken seriously and the Church as a whole body enabled to respond more effectively to society in the light of faith.

There are several strands to the argument. First, historically, power in the Church is seen to lie with the clergy; it is they who are perceived by most people to be the Church. Thus the 'concerns of the secular world will not actually be taken seriously by the Church unless some of its ordained office holders are active within secular affairs, and force the Church to pay attention to them. Conversely, the secular world will not actually perceive that the Church is committed to serve it and speak to its concerns if the Church is not prepared to ordain and thus commit its full authority to some who work entirely within it.'[6]

Secondly, work-focused non-stipendiary ministry would exhibit in a truly sacramental expression the essential principle of the Christian ministry. It would make clear that the ordained ministry is sustained by, as it is meant to 'perfect', that essential priesthood of all believers which embraces every legitimate vocation.[7] Thirdly, it would provide 'symbolic boundary people' in every area of life. Fourthly, it is a bridge, and as such assumes two-way traffic. Thus the authorised minister at work not only focuses publicly the Church's concerns in the work-place, but is also continuously accountable back to the Church for what he does there and is responsible for bringing that experience into the life of the whole Christian community.

CLERGY AND LAITY

The last fifteen to twenty years have seen a growing consciousness on the part of lay people that they are the Church. I mention just two ways in which this has manifested itself: first, the increasing demand for learning about the faith and for teaching of ministerial skills; and, secondly, the greater involvement and power of lay people in the government of the Church. This is partly seen in synodical government, but perhaps even more in reliance on the living Church for funding an ever-increasing proportion of clergy stipends, which brings with it the demand for accountability.

The issue of authority is central here too. For some lay people have become conscious that their skills and knowledge may count for something in the business of discovering what God is up to in the world, and that their Christian experience, wrought in many cases out of living in unsympathetic if not hostile environments, at work and in their local communities, may be every bit as valuable as the theological knowledge of the priest. Moreover, there has been theological teaching reinforcing this view. Study of the New Testament and Early Church reveals variety. The focusing of ministry in one man developed only over the first two centuries and obscured the earlier emphasis on a varied and more corporate expression of the ministry of the Church. The charismatic movement has made its contribution with its emphasis on the use of the gifts of each individual and 'every-member' ministry. It has enabled many people to become free of previously accepted authorities and traditions and to open themselves more fully to where the Holy Spirit is leading his Church. So where is authority to be found in the midst of all the different claims of Spirit, Christian experience, theological training, individual gifts and skills, ordination? What authority is it which is conferred by ordination?

What is being called into question here is not simply the role of the clergyman but the whole edifice of assumptions and expectations which has grown up around that role – views of the nature of theology; expectations about the clergy as the only possessors of theological knowledge, as the active partners with passive laity in the process of teaching and learning, preaching and listening, exercising and receiving pastoral care; assumptions about marked separations between spiritual and material, Church and world, religion and politics; and philosophies underpinning the training process.

What is undergoing change is the whole relationship between clergy and laity, and there is inevitably confusion and ambivalence, some anger and rebellion, and some evidence of a desire to retreat to safer and known ways of relating.

The development of non-stipendiary ministry needs to be seen in this context. There is real desire to be a bridge between clergy and laity, helping forward a new understanding of how authority may be handled and power expressed in the Christian community. There is also a desire to broaden the nature of the community by extending its horizons through direct and accountable experience of every aspect of life. Such a position is vulnerable because it rejects the comparative security of the professional club, while remaining open to the attacks of those who find threatening anything which does not fit into neat categories. No wonder so many find themselves pressed by the combined efforts of clergy and laity into more familiar and acceptable shapes.

VOCATION AND PROFESSIONALISM

Anthony Russell has charted the development of the clergyman as a professional together with the growth of an understanding of vocation as a calling to a role which was special and private. What had been legitimated by its place in the whole fabric of a Christian society was now located in the sacramental and spiritual nature of the Church.

There are two forces which lie behind the notions of 'vocation' and 'professionalism'. These sometimes conflict and sometimes work together. The first moves towards the idea of the life chosen for its rightness, if not for the love of it. The second emphasises the job to be done, draws boundaries and defines skills, and tends to support and maintain the existing order in the institution. Both of them, however, have encouraged a setting apart of the clergy from the laity and from society. The calling and skills of lay people are devalued, and by implication the relationship between God and his world is formalised. No wonder being ordained is so easily characterised as 'going into the Church'.

The development of a wider variety of formal and informal ministry calls into question our understandings of 'vocation' and 'professional'. Where we have non-stipendiary part-time ministers, lay and ordained, non-stipendiary full-time ministers, lay and ordained, people authorised at various levels for specific tasks, counselling, adult education, drama, hospital work, it becomes very much more difficult to talk about the professionalism only of the clergy.

Where we have an increasing awareness, not only that the call of an individual needs to be validated by a community, but that sometimes the community itself does the calling, then how can we talk about an individual feeling an internal call? For here vocation is something which emerges out of the relationship between individual and community and can have a very wide reference indeed. Non-stipendiary ministry is again part of this ferment, claiming a genuine calling to a ministry which may often be more appropriately validated by a person's local community than that of a stipendiary minister. Such a ministry can be just as professional in its approach, its framework of accountability and its theological and practical skills, even if all these differ from the ministry of a stipendiary minister.

SOME REFLECTIONS

I want to finish by trying to draw some threads together and then saying something more specifically about ordained ministry in secular employment. There are certain emphases which I think it is important to draw attention to.

The first is about the process of doing theology. It will be clear, I hope, from what I have said, that I do not believe that it is possible to define ordination or priesthood and proceed from there. These concepts, I suggest, have become so bound by the particular circumstances which gave birth to them that, if we are to free what they contain, we need to start with the situation which already exists and ask in what way they resonate with it. The consequences of this will be an approach which builds on the present situation with all its complex strands. Experiment, exploration and reflection upon it will be prominent, and it will have that fragmented and variegated character of which Ian Ramsey spoke in relation to theology in our time.[8] The point of coherence will be produced less by a uniformity of stance than by a commitment to respect and learn from different expressions within the total body.

The second is the need for an understanding of the Church in which the relationship between the Church and the world is seen in all its complexity and subtlety. History has demonstrated the tendency for that relationship to become frozen either in a union of Church and world or in their separation. But there is a dialectical unity that exists between Church and world and world and Church. It is a living relationship of constant change and interaction, and, from the Church's point of view, a high degree of dependency. 'In reality the Church does not dialogue with the world for the simple reason that she is not outside the world. She dialogues with the rest of the world, with the rest of humanity, since she herself is part of the world and part of humanity.'[9] Thus the tensions we find in the Church are reflections of those in the world. And it is through addressing the common human task in the world and all the tensions and conflicts which that involves that the Church evolves.

The third follows from this. It is natural for us to see the local Christian community in one dimension, and to identify it in terms of the people who meet together regularly in the same place. Yet the local Christian community is much more complex than that, for in the vast majority of cases it will be made up of several groups of people with different interests and experience. Somehow we need to help its members to become more conscious of their existence as a community with several dimensions and to find ways in which the eucharist they make together might reflect this with greater effectiveness and richness. Seen in this way the community might need to develop several modes of operation, focusing at different times on different areas of life which are significant for groups of its members, be they work, local community, national or international affairs, and involving different people in leading roles.

It is within these parameters that the ordination of those who see their ministry as primarily focused in their work-place needs to be seen.

If we are to come to see the Christian community as more than the parish family at the Lord's table on the Lord's day, and if the priesthood which properly belongs to the people of God is to be appropriately expressed, then work-focused NSM is just one of many ways in which the Church needs to authorise people for particular tasks.

Ordination in this sense is primarily to do with the conferring of authority, but it is authority for a role which has many resonances with the concept of priesthood as it has in the past developed. The ordained man in this position is a representative of Jesus Christ to the Christian community when they are operating in that mode which reflects work and industry. He is also a representative of Jesus Christ to the world in which he works, focusing the Church's concern and providing a symbol. Some would argue that this is a confusing symbol, because most people's understanding of the symbol of priesthood is that it goes with the full-time religious practitioner. But it has not been confusing in past periods of history where priests combined their priesthood with all kinds of secular jobs, from politics to farming. What is important is that we take people's symbolic life seriously and try to work with it in ways which give expression to how we now understand God's relationship with his world.

The Lima Text says at one point that 'in order to fulfil its mission, the Church needs persons who are publicly and continually responsible for pointing to its fundamental dependence on Jesus Christ, and thereby provide, within a multiplicity of gifts, a focus on his ministry.'[10] This *public* responsibility and accountability seems to me a central facet in the working out of the role of the ordained minister at work, and it is that which in the first instance marks him out as having a different role from the Christian lay person.

Another way in which his task resonates with the concept of individual priesthood is in relation to sacraments. Another effect of stressing the breadth of community consciousness which we need to develop, if we are to maintain the dialectical unity between a Church in the world and the world in the Church, is that people need to be helped to fill out the content of the sacraments within the Church with meanings and resonances from their everyday lives. Michael Ranken uses the analogy of the Church's experience of overseas mission in the last century, and asks us to take seriously the religious perceptions which already exist 'out there', 'even if they be expressed in forms which are strange to an evangelist who does not know the language or the customs of the country'.[11] One of the ordained person's tasks is to recognise these secular sacraments, to help those involved to use them for what they are, and to feed back into the sacramental life of the Christian community this richness of God's presence in his world. Schillebeeckx seems to be saying something similar when he says that 'secular and symbolic or liturgical forms of communicating meaning need one another and provoke one another. This means that the community, and thus its leaders, no longer locates the meaning of life and religious need so exclusively and so massively in the liturgy and the sacraments.'[12] The work-focused NSM has a central part to play in all this.

I want to emphasise again the importance of the corporate in relation to the calling and authorising of the NSM. We have been bedevilled for too long by an individualist approach which insists on detaching the individual priest from the relationship with the community. To quote the Lima Text again, 'ordained ministry has no existence apart from the community. They cannot dispense with the recognition, the support and the encouragement of the community. The authority of the ordained minister is not to be understood as the possession of the ordained person, but as a gift for the continuing edification of the body in and for which the minister has been ordained.'[13] This seems to me to be of vital importance in the development of work-focused NSM.

It is also necessary to see the exercise of ministry in communal and collegial terms with lay people, and with industrial chaplains, where they exist. The NSM is there to help others express the priesthood of the Church, giving some kind of recognisable leadership to his fellow Christians in their lay ministry, articulating the questions they ask and encouraging them to dig below the surface and face them at their true theological depth. He is also there to help them discover what worship might mean, and how it might be expressed. Industrial chaplains vary in the ways they approach their work, but clearly there will be cases where their role will have to change as they engage in collaborative ministry with NSMs, just as the ministry of stipendiary parish clergy has to change.

While I have in the end said something about NSM in the workplace, I have tried to emphasise that this question cannot really be looked at in isolation from much wider questions about Church and ministry, the existence of which in the Church at large have actually contributed to the rise of the NSM phenomenon. I am also aware that I have tried to develop just one model. Other models could have been developed, in which work-focused NSM would have had no valid place.

Meanwhile many NSMs have in the practice of their ministry to carry the burden of this wider questioning. But perhaps it is only through the experiences which arise from this practice, painful though some of them are, that the exploratory theology which is necessary can be done. It is a lonely task, defined by Michael Bourke as discovering what faith is, and what it means to be a disciple in the secular world, and to seek the 'Church' out there – without denying the traditional 'Church' back home;[14] and it is likely to take several generations before any real clarity emerges. It means that we shall need to go on listening sensitively to the expereience of the ministers themselves, for some time to come, as Patrick Vaughan has already set out to do.[15]

[1] Anthony Russell, *The Clerical Profession* (SPCK 1980), p. 262.
[2] E. Schillebeeckx, *Ministry: A Case for Change* (SCM Press 1981), p. 75.
[3] R. P. C. Hanson, *Christian Priesthood Examined* (Lutterworth 1979), p. 18.
[4] Bruce Reed, *The Dynamics of Religion* (Darton, Longman & Todd 1978), p. 215.
[5] See Mary Douglas, *Natural Symbols* (Penguin 1978) and Edmund Leach, *Culture and Communication* (CUP 1976), esp. ch. 7.
[6] Michael Bourke, 'The Theology of Non-Stipendiary Ministry', *Theology*, vol. LXXXIV, May 1981, pp. 177–82.
[7] F. R. Barry, *The Relevance of the Church* (Nisbet 1935), pp. 206–19.
[8] I. T. Ramsey in *Towards a Theology of Education*, Bloxham Project Conference, 1972.
[9] J. L. Segundo, *The Community called Church* (Orbis 1973), p. 70.
[10] 'Baptism, Eucharist and Ministry', *International Review of Mission*, vol. LXXII, p. 182.

[11] Michael Ranken, 'A Theology for the Priest at Work', *Theology,* vol. LXXV, March 1982, pp. 108–13.

[12] E. Schillebeeckx, op. cit., p. 137.

[13] 'Baptism, Eucharist and Ministry', loc. cit.

[14] Michael Bourke, loc. cit.

[15] See Chapter III below.

III SPEAKING FOR THEMSELVES

At the end of his chapter on 'NSM in Context', Robert Langley referred to research recently undertaken by Patrick Vaughan, in the course of which he had encouraged non-stipendiary ministers, who were exercising a ministry at work, to reflect and articulate for themselves how they understood their ministry and what seemed to them to be its special nature and function. In this chapter Patrick Vaughan draws upon that research, summarises its findings and points up some of the lessons that may be learned from it.

Traditionally the ordained ministry of the Church of England has been exercised within the structure of the parochial system, or through sector ministry in schools, hospitals, prisons, etc. But over the last decade the existence of ordained ministers in secular employment in the fields of commerce, industry and local government has offered the possibility of a new style of ministry: ministry 'in the world of work'. This has been hailed by some as 'a reinterpretation of the whole nature of ministry'.[1] Others have taken a more critical view, fearing that 'the engagement of the Church with the world through the laity could be obscured'.[2]

In this debate, surprisingly little attempt has been made to discover exactly what ministry in the world of work might be. Discussion of the subject has usually been dominated by concepts derived from parochial ministry, which has made it difficult for many NSMs to enunciate their particular insights about ministry. They are constantly hounded by questions like "Why do you need to be ordained to bear Christian witness at work? Doesn't your baptism authorise you to do that?' or 'What more are you doing at work now that you are ordained?' It is virtually impossible to answer these questions in terms of the questioner's assumptions. Such questions are inappropriate, because they tacitly assume the parochial model as normative, and require NSMs to justify themselves in terms of the parochial minister's language. But these terms seem foreign to work-focused NSMs, who prefer to choose their own.

What might these terms be? To answer this question, I undertook a small research project[3] in 1983, interviewing eleven NSMs in the East Midlands region.

The interview focused around two themes: stories and roles. I invited the NSMs to tell me 'stories or incidents which will illustrate ways in which you practise your ministry in the world of work'. Having listened to these stories I then invited the NSMs to state what roles they perceived themselves to have been playing in each story, and what it was about the nature of the job which enabled or excluded certain roles.

What emerged was fascinating. All in turn were apologetic that they had not much to say (and in terms of traditional expressions of ministry that was true), but they had no difficulty in producing stories illustrating a recognisable ministry. When they were collected together I found that certain kinds of story tended to recur.

Before turning to an analysis of them, it may be helpful to explain who my respondents were. One was self-employed (a pharmacist); two were teachers; two worked for a local authority (in careers and transport); two for the Health Service (a consultant and a secretary); and four in industry (two engineers, a company representative, and a training manager). All were professional people, often at middle management level. These social factors undoubtedly influenced the opportunities for ministry available to them. Five were in priest's orders, five in deacon's orders, and one a deaconess. They had exercised ordained ministry for periods ranging between one and four years.

THE STYLE OF MINISTRY

The stories which I elicited inevitably included many examples of pastoral ministry to individual colleagues at work. Many stories proffered were of people seeking counsel about personal (often family) problems, where the NSM was cast in the role of informal counsellor or listener.

Very often, too, the NSM was treated as a public relations person for the Church, as an ecclesiastical information bureau. Thus NSMs were often approached with questions about the Church's regulations regarding remarriage, and with requests that the NSM might conduct or take part in a baptism, marriage or funeral. It was often apparent that the NSM was the only ordained person known to unchurched work colleagues. The NSM thus clearly acted as a link person or bridge person when such unchurched people needed or wanted some ecclesiastical information or service. Stories of the above kind were plentiful and did not need prompting. They conform pretty closely to the kind of things expected of parochial clergy, and will not, therefore, be discussed in detail here.

However, another kind of response to my question was to tell of an incident, often a very brief one, which the teller considered to be 'ministry'. One NSM described this as 'the five-minute ministry'. It consisted of a brief conversation, of an apparently ordinary nature, which in some way took a turn which was perceived to be 'important', because a significant meeting took place. For instance:

> My boss on being greeted conventionally, 'How are you?', replied flippantly, with an answer implying you had to be on good form in this job. 'No, how are *you*?', I repeated. The boss stopped on his way down the stairs, when he realised I was genuinely asking about *him*. He took hold of the fact that the question was meant genuinely. He said there were personal difficulties. No further than that. But in saying that, he sort of unburdened himself. For one moment we got under the outer image. I was concerned for him, knowing of his previous heart attack.

One NSM recounted a story when he perceived himself to have 'a ministry of punctuation' – dotting the 'i's and crossing the 't's of another's journey:

> A charge nurse went out of his way in the corridor to say he had gone back to church after an absence of many years, and was clearly bubbling over with enthusiasm to tell me. I felt he *wanted* to tell me. He was thus able to take the experience he had had in the church and anchor it into his everyday experience by sharing it with someone at work who could approve it. I was saying 'It's OK'. He singled me out because I have a two-fold authority both in the secular job and in the church.

As each story was told, I asked the NSMs to identify in their own words what role they had been playing in the story. Very few of the answers given were specifically religious: the word 'priest' was never used. Answers included being a Listener, Counsellor, Reflector, Sharer, Ecclesiastical Information Bureau, a Friendly Christian, being available, being a person of integrity. Most of the stories recounted typical human situations where the NSM was being no more than a caring, thoughtful, wise or loving human being.

18

FACILITATING OR LIMITING FACTORS

A position of authority can be an advantage because it allows scope for leadership and personal choice of style of leadership. Many NSMs were in middle management positions and had a certain amount of control of their use of time and movements. Several cited accessibility in a known office or desk to be valuable. Others equated the requirements of good management and Christian ministry. One said that the fact that he had been in his job a long time meant he didn't have to establish credibility:

> They know me well enough to know my credibility is sound – almost as if to say 'Well, if W says it is so, then there must be something in it; if W thinks this, it's got to be worth thinking about'.

On the other hand, the limitations imposed on ministry by the job situation were firmly stated. One must not waste the firm's time by engaging in lengthy conversations unconnected with work. The performance at one's job must not decline. A manager who controls much of his own time said:

> People's eyes are on you. They also have 'extra-mural' activities. If I were seen to be skipping off too often in mid-afternoon to take various functions, it would be an undermining of the authority of management and relationships between staff.

The hierarchy of roles at work clearly places limits on ministry. Several people spoke of the undesirability of jumping across well-recognised status divisions in an attempt to minister. This may well mean that because of existing authority structures it is impossible for NSMs to minister to those immediately beneath them. Any such attempted gesture will probably be doomed to failure; it will not be easy for the junior colleague to receive it; moreover subsequent working relations may be confused, and perhaps impaired.

Several people spoke of the difficulty NSMs find when their management role requires them to discipline someone. There are bound to be conflict situations. One NSM described the dilemma of 'this schizophrenic thing' of being both priest and manager:

> You are known as a priest and therefore have to be very careful when you are disciplining people, because you have got to care for the person. You may have to take someone to task because the result of their ineffectiveness is that other people in the organisation are suffering, or not getting the lead they should have; but you have still got to regard the integrity of that person when you are taking them down a peg or two. He's got to be able to

walk away feeling he is still a man. I find that very difficult. I've been greatly encouraged on the two occasions I have had to do it, when, on both occasions, the staff concerned have come to me afterwards and thanked me for the careful way in which it has been handled, and the regard I have had for their feelings and sensitivities – whilst at the same time leaving them in no doubt as to how I felt about their performance. One has separated the performance from the person.

PERCEIVED ROLES

Halfway through the interview, I threw in a prompting checklist of eight possible roles for NSMs at work, prepared by the Church in Wales.[4] I asked each one to say which roles they themselves played often, which seldom and which never. The roles most frequently reported as often performed were Interpreter and Intercessor (9) and Teacher (8). Those least performed were Confessor (5 seldom, 6 never) and Nucleus (2 often, 1 seldom, 8 never). Other roles were fairly evenly spread.

Having seen this list, the minds of respondents were then stimulated to produce further stories. In many cases they merely amplified earlier stories, but in two significant cases (Intercessor and Confessor) totally new kinds of story emerged. What was surprising was that the ministry of Intercessor did not emerge at all in the unprompted earlier stories, although practically everyone on seeing the list acknowledged its frequency. One respondent on being asked, 'Would the role of Intercessor be common?', replied excitedly, 'It would, it would, and I hadn't realised it counted!' He went on to say: 'It is surprising how people will ask me to pray for them. People will phone me up and say "So and so is happening: will you say a prayer for me?"'

Another NSM has an unwritten contract with several other Christians at work that they will privately pray for situations and people they are dealing with. Another keeps an intercession list in a notebook, with names of everyone he sees in the course of a week's case-load.

> It does not mean actually naming everyone – just taking hold of the book and knowing that it is there. I think that's OK. Each Sunday before the parish Eucharist I pick out one or two I'm most concerned about, write their names on a little card and put it on the altar so they are taken into the Eucharist with us.

20

The same person told of their practice of praying while working:

> The Jesus Prayer is the key prayer. One can allow it to well up. I find when
> I am listening to people, I am also praying the Jesus Prayer.

The other role surprisingly revealed by the checklist was of Confessor.
Several people cited situations in which they perceived themselves
informally to be speaking of repentance and forgiveness:

> It normally happens when people are feeling bad about having let
> someone down. My response is 'Never mind. Explain what happened.
> They'll forgive you.'

Although several NSMs told stories of being asked to conduct
occasional offices in church, for workmates or their families, only one
NSM said he had a liturgical ministry at work. He regularly wore his
clerical collar at school, where he had initiated a weekly lunch-hour
Eucharist and two other weekly periods of prayer. Most other
respondents said they did not think it appropriate to play the role of
nucleus for Christian groups at work. Reasons given for this stance
were that Christian prayer groups at work tended to be exclusive, and
often of an (uncongenial) fundamentalist character; and that the
lunch break was very short. Typical of the rationale against playing
this role of nucleus is this comment:

> If I formed a cell within —— I could become quite elitist and exclusive
> and might well destroy what I am trying to do, which is just to be amongst
> it all. I happen to think it has much more validity to be available to 150
> people at lunchtime than to be in a nice little group somewhere.

These are the basic facts that emerge from working through the
questionnaire with eleven NSMs. However, in the course of relating
their stories and incidents about ministry at work, four special issues
frequently emerged which are worth separate consideration.

PERCEPTION OF THE EFFECT OF ORDINATION

Many of those interviewed were apologetic that they could not
produce many stories of ministry at work, and considered that what
they did tell me were small and insignificant things, which might very
well have happened whether or not they were ordained. Nevertheless,
two people spoke of a dramatic increase in the frequency of these
small incidents. One, an industrialist, who had been known as a
committed Christian for a long time, said:

21

I can't recall any of these situations happening before. What ordination did for me was twofold. The training for it equipped me to a certain level, and gave me insight into a whole range of things concerned with human relations. Secondly, the fact of ordination brought this knowledge to the attention of a whole lot of people. People search me out now, and bring things to me that they never did before.

The official and public nature of ordination is clearly valued not only by the NSMs but by the work organisations;:

The director of Marketing mentioned my ordination at a London meeting. To which the Sales Manager at —— responded with evident local pride 'It's one of our blokes from the East Midlands that's doing this.'

When ordination is thus valued by the work organisation, increased confidence obviously arises in NSMs and this is coupled with the confidence offered by the Church's own acknowledgment of them. Reflecting on this, one NSM industrialist, whose job includes meeting his staff individually for annual counselling and appraisal, said:

I am now finding a much closer relationship with my own staff at work, because they seem to feel they can be much more open with me. It is my ordination which gives an aura of trust and confidentiality. Staff are more willing to go into private areas of their lives – which they wouldn't do with a boss at work. They have found the fact that I have been ordained has made for a much better working relationship.

Many stories indicate the initiative taken by others in approaching NSMs. The fact that the NSM is a 'marked' Christian has had the effect of giving confidence to other Christians at work.

A dramatic instance is provided by an industrialist whose job required him to move to another office. In the space of a few years he was astonished to find the same phenomenon happening twice over:

It happened first at —— on announcing my intention to train for non-stipendiary ministry. A colleague jokingly commented, 'That will bring fresh meaning to the terminology "prayer meeting"' (work jargon for Managers' meeting). Then people began to talk amongst themselves. A Roman Catholic girl (whose religion was unknown to me) came and said, 'For the first time, because you are doing this, I can talk openly. I've always been afraid to mention I was a Catholic.' Gradually, people began to sport fish badges, and little crosses on their lapels. One man was a churchwarden and a district engineer, who had never done so before. In —— the same thing happened. People began to call in to the office and talk about it, and to ask me to pray for people and situations. And again people would have fish badges or crosses on their lapels. It wouldn't have been quite the same if I had been a labourer or a draughtsman. Some of it was the position I hold. It is as though people say to themselves 'If he says its alright, and if he is not frightened to admit openly that he is a Christian, then it must be alright for me.'

PERCEPTION OF THE JOB

Several NSMs perceived their very jobs to be ministry. They derived this perception from a particular world-affirming theology. 'Christian life is normal life, ordinary life, life in its fullness', said one. Consequently a high standard of job performance is the essence.

> Ministry at work is not overt. It starts with the manner in which you do your job. My Christian witness in the office (very much like anybody else) is proclaimed by how well I do my professional job of being the transport officer.

It so happens that many NSMs hold jobs in middle or senior management, where the work is about handling people whether as individual staff or as groups. It is fascinating to listen to NSMs' theological interpretation of their job requirements. One whose work revolves around negotiations with other companies said:

> The nature of the job requires me to be a bridge-person. The job involves persuading various companies to co-operate, therefore the whole thing revolves around a network of relationships. The job itself is mediatorial. There is a wide overlap between the nature of this job and the nature of 'priestly' ministry – though I wouldn't want to imply that others didn't also have a priestly ministry. Isn't there something priestly about being a managing director, pulling people together?

Another NSM echoed the very same perception:

> The management role has a lot of priest-like qualities about it, if it is good management. If a manager is doing his job, conscious of God's action or not, he will be looking after his staff, enabling them and counselling them.

Another NSM who is in senior management in a very person-oriented organisation said:

> A lot of management is to do with working together – co-operation rather than dictation. This influences my management style because I don't think I will get commitment from people to ideas and practices unless they are part of the decision-making process. And I believe that this is good theological as well as good psychological practice. The technical words to describe it may be different, but the principles you are describing are the same.

He went on to instance ways in which his Christian perceptions influence his management style:

I always write when illnesses or bereavements are notified. I would have done this anyway, before ordination. In management terms it has to be good to demonstrate that one is taking an interest in the whole person and not just regarding them as a working unit. But there is now an element of expectation by staff – expecting a priest to take an interest at such times. My work is my parish. I try to ensure that slightly more than normal courtesies are observed. I take time to drop notes of thanks and encouragement. I take time to meet people, and encourage good things that they are doing.

One of the NSMs interviewed had a markedly different perception of his job. On being asked whether there was an overlap between his job as a teacher and his Christian ministry, he replied:

I don't know. The job itself is irrelevant. All the job does is put me in touch with certain groups of people. They see me as a sort of Lay Preacher; therefore any concept of Priest as I see it is denied them, because they don't know it exists. It could easily degenerate into school counsellor. If that happened, I should not thereby by enabled to work as a priest, because it would be seen as indoctrination. I'd much rather 'be there', so that people can come openly and willingly – in which case they come on my terms.

This NSM's understanding of his job is in stark contrast to those cited above. The difference seems to be related to his self-image. He decided to wear clerical dress at school from the day of his ordination, and saw his ministry as a priest (his phrase) solely in liturgical terms. He perceived it to be his duty to develop such occasions as a weekly eucharist for staff and pupils. Only a small number attended these services. He said he could not see his teaching role itself to be ministry. He acknowledged he had never played the roles of counsellor, confessor, comforter or reconciler at work. Much of what he stood for seemed to be rejected by colleagues and pupils. It seems difficult to resist the conclusion that in this case the dominant parochial model of ministry had been transported into school, and that the school environment was decisively rejecting it as inappropriate.

PERCEPTIONS ABOUT ISSUES AT WORK

Several NSMs told stories about how they had directly or indirectly ministered to the structures of their organisations by encouraging deeper thinking about work-related issues.

24

One NSM is an officer of the national committee of his professional association. By chance conversations he has discovered that several other officials in the association are committed Christians. He recounted how, at the national council conference ball, he was introduced by one of' these officials to the head of another large company who was concerned how he, as a top man in industry, could exercise his Christian understanding. So on the edge of the dance floor a deep conversation ensued! Now an informal circle of Christian leaders of that industry exchange letters and papers, grappling with issues such as unemployment. The general aim is to reduce the work force. But that begs the question (for the concerned Christian manager) of what he is going to do for the human beings concerned; how can he make management decisions based on an ethic which has Christianity at its heart? How can he cope with the human aspects of a policy of labour reduction? Through informal exchange of ideas through papers and over lunch, the geographically isolated members of this small circle are affirming each other's Christian concern and action. The NSM is but one member of the circle, playing his part alongside committed laymen.

PERCEPTIONS OF THE WORK – PARISH RELATIONSHIP
Because of the practice of licensing NSMs to particular parishes, every NSM interviewed also had a parochial ministry alongside the ministry at work. None of them gave the slightest sign of resentment of the parochial connection. On the contrary, it was highly valued.

As has already been noted, the role of Interpreter was the most frequently identified NSM role. This role is two-faced: as an interpreter of the Church to the world (at work) and of the world to the Church (in the congregation). Respondents' comments indicated three kinds of instance where this work experience directly provided opportunities for ministry in the parochial setting: in teaching situations (church meetings), in sermons, and in pastoral contacts (e.g. baptism preparation). In addition, the presence of NSMs in clergy chapter meetings can be important for educating the parochial clergy. NSMs also perceive that the pressures they share in the world of work both with the unchurched and with the Christian laity provide them with an empathy denied to parochial clergy.

However, the tensions produced within NSMs through their parochial ministry can be very real. The attractiveness of parochial

25

ministry can be experienced as a seductive lure, as the following powerful and emotive statement makes clear:

> The Daily Office before work has been wonderful to me – the peace and quiet and the *joint* prayer with the incumbent. This can be all very disturbing. You feel 'This is great! Why am I involved in all that hassle? What is it about?' It can be quite demotivating! I can arrive in the office, and I just don't want to know, I feel so full of the glory of God. I feel it's pointless: I've got to go to this meeting and I've got to get all wound up about this particular point – and it *doesn't really matter*!

The 'hassle' referred to above is the fourfold demand of the job, church, family and the need for re-creation. What it feels like to live constantly with this hassle is well expressed in the following statement:

> Everything is alright as long as everything is alright! By which I mean I can cope with both sides as long as I'm confident and competent in what I am doing from the church point of view. Take preaching: if I'm on top of my job and have prepared the sermon, I can go out and be fulfilled and enjoy it. I'm alright. But if I haven't had proper time for sermon preparation I can reach Monday morning again, and I'm in quite a state, because I've had no relaxation over the week-end. There are phases when I'm uptight with work and then I can't somehow cope with home. I can quite understand the tensions with NSMs who eventually go full-time.

WHAT ARE THESE NSMs SAYING TO THE CHURCH?

The great value of having invited NSMs to tell stories of situations where they have perceived ministry to be happening, is that is has allowed them to choose their own terms. They have not felt obliged to use traditional priestly or ecclesiastical language. Listening to the stories with a well-tuned ear, we may hear truths which have become smothered beneath the dominant language of parochial ministry. These may well be truths which the whole Church needs to hear.

(a) *The essence of 'ministry'*

Many of the stories seem to be describing very ordinary human situations. And they seem to be reminding us that on the one hand Christian ministry is no more (or no less!) than a very ordinary and natural human encounter. But on the other hand, paradoxically, the same stories seem to be saying that these encounters are extra-ordinary, in the sense that they are perceived to be unusually 'important' (and perhaps infrequent). One further case illustrates this very clearly. An NSM who works as a secretary in a medical unit was invited to give a brief paper on the spiritual life of the unit to a staffs conference. In it she said:

> I suggest that the spiritual life of the Unit is quite often hidden and goes largely unrecognised even by the people concerned. I think it is revealed when any member of staff sees the patient in front of him or her as a *person* – recognises the essential core of that person, the spirit – and relates on that level, as one human being to another. This is happening all the time in a very simple way.
>
> I was talking recently.to one of our patients who said that she had been very apprehensive at coming to —— the second time. The first time it had not proved possible to carry out a minor operation to help her and she was very afraid the same thing would happen again. The feeling of apprehension had lasted until she saw a young nurse whose face had lit up as she called her by name and said 'Oh, how nice it is to see you again.' The patient said that she had suddenly felt like a human being and not like somebody who just occupied a bed. I think that that young nurse, in meeting the woman's unspoken need, had, quite unconsciously, been a channel for the love of God.

This evoked much comment afterwards from the nursing staff, who seemed 'delighted that I was seeing them like that'. A consultant was heard to remark 'This has made me feel I walk around the Unit with my eyes closed.'

This story contains elements of both the ordinariness and the extra-ordinariness of Christian ministry. The incident of the greeting is very ordinary. But the fact that she had perceived it as a channel of God's love, had had the courage to cite it, and had been given the opportunity to do so – not to mention the response of the unit's staff – are all extra-ordinary. This kind of story reminds the Church that 'the real presence of Christ' is readily found in the world of work, and that preaching does not require a pulpit.

(b) *The nature of ordination*

But what makes the extra-ordinary possible? Many stories seem to say quite clearly that it is the fact of ordination. Interestingly, the stories did not allude in any way to the 'grace of orders'. The points being made were much more pragmatic. They had had training, which gave them access to new knowledge, to new ways of looking at things. Moreover, it marked them publicly as representatives of the Church, and this in turn seems to have given them a new confidence in their own perceptions and convictions.

Such observations raise important questions about the most appropriate way in which to discuss ordination. Theological discussion of ordination commonly focuses on concepts of 'priesthood', but this was a word which was used only very occasionally by our respondents. They apparently preferred to discuss the subject in other terms. This phenomenon is all the more intriguing, since several respondents belonged to distinctly Catholic traditions.

Most commonly the matter was raised in relation to the 'authority' conferred by ordination. But ordination to what? The respondents belonged to three distinct orders – deaconess, deacon and priest. Yet it was impossible to distinguish from their replies who belonged to which order. Indeed in one case it appears that, while he was an ordinand in training, one respondent had had ordained authority imputed to him. This phenomenon is worthy of attention. The significant features of ordained status are seen to be the preliminary training, the public authorisation, the assumed skills and insights. These features fall into sociological rather than theological categories. Can it be that the most satisfactory statements about ordination are sociological ones, rather than theological ones?

(c) 'Standard-bearers' accepted

Many stories showed how 'outsiders' in the world value the presence of an ordained person. To use a gospel metaphor, it seems that this marked Christian presence acts like salt, bringing out the good savour which is potentially in the food, but which is not apparent until drawn out by the salt. Conversely, other stories show how 'insiders' (members of the Christian community) are encouraged in their Christian witness at work by an ordained presence. So far from justifying the fears that a priest at work de-skills the laity, our stories suggest the opposite. They clearly indicate that the witness of Christian laity at work can be strengthened by the presence of an NSM. The NSM seems to function like the standard-bearer in a medieval battle: in the mêlée and confusion of the fight, troops caught sight of the lofty standard and rallied there. The many stories of previously unknown Christians 'coming out' seem to justify this analogy.

In these various ways, the NSM thus seems to become a focal person both for 'outsiders' and 'insiders'. What is interesting is that in most cases this happens without the NSM exercising any liturgical function at work. Whereas traditional ecclesial thinking about priesthood typically locates the essence of priesthood in presiding at the eucharist, these stories seem to be speaking of truly mediatorial, representative and pastoral activities without any formal altar. It seems that these NSMs find no difficulty in discovering ways of celebrating the 'secular sacraments' that Michael Austin has provocatively postulated.[5]

(d) *Ecclesial roles rejected*

If it is true that the world of work is open to receive the ministry of 'secular sacraments', it is also quite clear from the stories that it is not willing to receive overtly ecclesial sacraments. These are seen to be inappropriate, out of place or even unprofessional in the world of work. Time is too short for a eucharist at lunch-break, which in any case ought more appropriately to be a time to relax before the afternoon's work. Overt evangelising would upset working relations. For the psychiatrist to practise formal absolution in the hospital would be 'unprofessional'.

(e) *'Kingdom' theology fundamental*

Many stories indicate that the speaker held a world-affirming view of life. Incarnational theology had been fully imbibed and become a part of the NSM's world view. Basically the stories seem to insist that the arena of God's activity is the world, not just the Church. This emphasis must surely be a healthy counterpart to the message conveyed by many clergy activities. Parochial clergy usually feel themselves to be charged with 'running the congregation' and devote much energy to 'getting people involved' in church affairs. Necessary as these activities may be, they cannot be identified with 'making ready for the kingdom of God'.

NSMs are thus enriching the total ministry of the Church, since they are inevitably more representative of the people of God (the laity) than are the full-time paid professionals. The latter, by virtue of their stipend (i.e. being paid in order not to need secular employment) are denied an 'ordinary' working experience, and thus do not and cannot *in their persons* represent the world of secular work. The existence of secularly employed ordained persons is thus symbolically a deep enrichment to the Church.

29

(f) *Parochial links valued*

In saying this, however, it is important to stress that the stories do not suggest that the NSMs see themselves over against the parochial ministry. All were licensed to parish churches, and all deeply valued this deliberate institutional association with one particular worshipping community. The fact that as individuals they enjoy sharing in a small way in the traditional ministries around altar, pulpit and font, clearly indicates that these NSMs did not polarise their ministry with that of the parochial clergy. They perceived a continuity of ministry running between their ecclesiastical ministrations and the work of their secular employment. The continuity was vested in their own persons. Indeed without the opportunity to function within the liturgy of the Christian community on Sundays, their presence as ordained ministers in the world of work could scarcely be authentic.

(g) *Theologising by story-telling*

This project, with its small sample, cannot claim to be representative of NSMs as a whole. It does, however, claim to reveal that, despite the paucity of published material, theological reflection on NSM is far from absent in the Church, and that it may be effectively expressed through the medium of story-telling. If NSMs were regularly to tell their incumbents the kind of stories they have related to me, the parochial clergy would quickly perceive the extent to which NSMs are exercising Christian ministry at the frontier. They would become more ready to offer meaningful support, and less inclined to overburden 'good and faithful servants' with parochial busy-ness.

I remain indebted to the eleven NSMs who told me their stories: I found it a deeply moving experience to be entrusted with some very personal reflections.

[1] Anthony Russell, *The Clerical Profession* (SPCK 1980), p. 278.
[2] E. R. Wickham, in D. L. Edwards, ed., *Priests and Workers* (SCM 1961), p. 146.
[3] *How do Non-Stipendiary Ministers Perceive the Nature of their Ministry in the World of Work?*, a Research Project prepared for the Mid-Service Clergy Course XXVIII, July 1983, at St George's House, Windsor Castle.
[4] *Report to the Bench of Bishops of the Working Group on the Self-Supporting Ministry*, Church in Wales Publications 1981. The checklist included the following eight possible roles:
   (a) an *interpreter* of the Church to the world, and of the world to the Church;
   (b) an informal *teacher*, in down-to-earth theology and ethics;
   (c) a *counsellor* with an understanding of problems born of shared experience;

(d) a *confessor*, speaking wisely of repentance and forgiveness;

(e) a *comforter* to the distressed and bereaved;

(f) a *reconciler* between man and God and between different people, whether as individuals or groups;

(g) an *intercessor* who prays for all with whom and for whom he works;

(h) the *nucleus* for Christian groups.

⁵ Michael Austin, 'Towards a Secular Ministry', *The Modern Churchman*, Winter 1979, pp. 156–66.

IV MINISTERS OF THE KINGDOM

In discussing ordained ministry exercised at work Patrick Vaughan has stressed the importance of a 'kingdom' theology, and it is in keeping with this insight that we might think of non-stipendiary ministers as in some sense 'ministers of the kingdom'. In this chapter I propose to spell out in somewhat greater detail what this insight means.

In an essay entitled 'Kingdom, Church and Ministry', John Robinson wrote: 'Just as the New Testament bids us have as high a doctrine of the ministry as we like, as long as our doctrine of the Church is higher, so it commands us have as high a doctrine of the Church as we may, provided our doctrine of the Kingdom is higher.'[1] This understanding of things is of fundamental importance. If we fail to keep to this order of priorities, the clergy are in danger of seeming to be the *real* Christians – it is they who have 'gone into the Church'! – while the Church is in danger of seeming to be the place where God is *really* present, while the world is reduced to no more than a stage on which the drama of redemption is played out or, even more darkly, to the domain of Satan and his angels. If, however, we maintain this order of priorities, then ministry is exercised through the Church and on behalf of the Church – it is the Church which 'calls' persons to be its ministers, and, like Ambrose or Augustine, these persons may sometimes experience an initial reluctance to respond to this 'vocation' – and the Church, though not to be identified with the kingdom, is nevertheless a sign and instrument of God's kingdom, pointing to it wherever it manifests itself and participating in it in the present through faith and anticipating its future coming in hope.

A 'kingdom theology' might be expected to embody some or all of the following assumptions. First, it is the whole family of humankind, indeed the whole created order, rather than any one special, restricted portion of it, which is the object of God's continuing creative, redemptive and fulfilling love. 'God so loved *the world,* that he gave his only Son, that *whosoever* should believe in him should not perish but have life eternal.' This cosmic emphasis is to be found more frequently in eastern than in western theology. Indeed it might be said to find expression also in eastern rather than western church architecture. Whereas a typical western church looks like a fortress, offering safety and protection from the hostile elements without, a typical eastern church, with its onion-shaped spire which, I believe, really represents a flower of paradise, suggests that through the Church's ministry the garden of the world with all its thorns and thistles may once again be transformed into the paradise which it was originally intended to be.

Secondly, there are men and women co-operating with the creative, redemptive and fulfilling will of God even though they do not recognise the fact and may not even believe in God. We may think of such men and women, if we like, as 'anonymous Christians' or as those whose 'faith is known to God alone'. Alternatively, we need not use the language of Christian faith at all, and simply refer to them as 'men and women of good will'. Even in a world that is corrupted through and through by sin, it is possible for human beings to respond openly and unselfishly to the presence and appeal of the true, the beautiful and the good, themselves signs and expressions of God's kingdom.

Thirdly, the Church is that part of God's creation where the reality of the divine love is recognised, acknowledged, celebrated, proclaimed, and professed. Such a view has been powerfully expressed by W. H. Vanstone in his deeply perceptive and moving book, *Love's Endeavour, Love's Expense*: 'The Church occupies the enclave of recognition within the area of freedom: it is all within the area of freedom which would not be if the love of God were not recognised as love: it is all that is done to articulate awareness of the Creator's love.'[2] A not dissimilar thought was voiced by Karl Barth. The Christian is one who sees in the world 'the universal lordship of God, of the God who is the Father, who is the Father to him, his Father . . . He is simply made real by what he sees. And as such he is simply availing himself of a permission and invitation. He is going through an open door, but one which he himself has not opened, into a banqueting hall. And there he willingly takes his place under the table, in the company of publicans, in the company of beasts and plants and stones, accepting solidarity with them, being present simply as they are, as a creature of God,'[3] In a similar vein Barth awarded Mozart 'a place in theology especially in the doctrine of creation and also in eschatology . . . He had heard, and causes those who have ears to hear, even to-day, what we shall not see until the end of time – the whole context of providence. As though in the light of this end, he heard the harmony of creation to which the shadow also belongs but in which the shadow

33

is not darkness, deficiency is not defect, sadness cannot become despair, trouble cannot degenerate into tragedy and infinite melancholy is not ultimately forced to claim undisputed sway.'[4] Thus a theology of the Kingdom rejects all forms of dualism which make good and evil equal and ultimate forces, oppose spirit to matter, this world to the next. The temptation of such a theology is, perhaps, to fail to do justice to the sinfulness of sin and the evil of evil, and to play down a theology of redemption in favour of a theology of creation. A theology of the kingdom firmly maintains that the kingdom is the work and gift of God, not the achievement of human beings: it is for human beings to prepare for its coming and to be ready to receive it. Moreover, the kingdom will not be fully established in history as we know it: it is transcendent in origin and destiny. Nevertheless, nature and history are not untouched by the powers of the kingdom. In their processes God too is at work, continually creating and restoring, letting go and calling back, bringing good out of evil. The process by which God exercises his kingship includes both the possibility and the reality of what Barth calls 'the shadow'.

Fourthly, the 'reality' of the Christian in the world, whether we are thinking of the individual or of the whole people of God, is a reality of being, since to be an 'inheritor of the kingdom of God', something that is sacramentally signed in baptism, to receive a new identity, is to become a new person rather than to acquire a new possession. The recognition of and response to the love of God gives a person a new *centre* to his being, and so a new being. 'There is a new creation.' This does not decry or destroy the old creation, but it does transform it. And the essential work of ministry of the Church is to witness to his new creation. In a Lenten pastoral letter Cardinal Suhard of Paris once wrote: 'It is a good thing if priests become witnesses once more, less to conquer than to be a "sign". It has been well said that to bear witness to God does not mean to make propaganda, nor to evoke violent emotion, but rather "to keep the mystery of God present to men". But this means so to live that one's life would be inexplicable if God did not exist.'[5]

The world in which Christians are called to witness to God is, objectively speaking, an ambiguous world, a mixture of potentialities for good and evil and consequently open to more than one interpretation. In theological language, it is a created but fallen world. To speak in this way is not necessarily to subscribe to the belief that there was once a time when the world was not fallen, nor to the belief that all that is wrong with the world is ultimately due to the disobedience of the first human beings. It is, rather, to assert that God cares about man's total well-being, physical, mental and spiritual; that in creating the world he lets it be, giving it its own space and time and its own relative autonomy; and that in going its own way it 'gets it wrong' as often as (more often than?) it 'gets it right'. The processes of creation are hazardous, even when the creator is God.

At the natural level, things come into being and pass out of being within an interacting and interdependent system of energy, the pattern of which is experimentally determined, and those things survive and persist which adapt themselves to this environment. At the human level an analogous pattern is to be found. Self-interest and a sense of solidarity lead through conflict and co-operation either to an ordered system of justice and peace, in which individuals' rights and duties are acknowledged, or to injustice and warfare, in which the arbiter is force rather than persuasion. Where reason prevails, experiment and experience promote understanding and, on the basis of what has been found to be the case in the past, an element of prediction and control becomes possible for the future. There is no universal law of progress or decline, but rather a variable pattern of creation and destruction in which neither the light nor the darkness seems to predominate.

Thus at the human level the processes of history are, anthropologically and theologically, ambiguous. Individuals need to persist in their own individuality if they are to survive, but at the same time they need to be set free from egoistic self-awareness if they are to establish communities of trust and co-operation. The structures of government which the pursuit of a common good requires may themselves become the structures of oppression. Understanding based on past experience gives grounds for reasonable decision and action, but such understanding can itself become a blind guide unless it is balanced by an openness to the as yet untried potentialities of the future. The rights and duties recognised in a system of justice and equity are the prerequisite of any society that can claim to be civilised, but in the more personal relationships which are at the heart of human existence fairness is no substitute for love, nor can enlightened self-interest take the place of compassion and self-sacrifice.

From the point of view of a theology of the kingdom one of the functions of the Church is to witness to this ambiguity in human life and history, and to enable others also to recognise it for what it is.

Such recognition will not lead to its immediate elimination: the ambiguity is too deep-rooted for that to happen. But it may make it possible to confess and contain the ambiguity; and through faith in God confession and penitence can lead to new endurance, perseverance and hope. An example of this kind of ministry by the Church is to be found in the provision of special services of celebration for secular bodies, many if not all of which are inextricably involved, for better, for worse, in the ambiguities of human life. Such services should not be designed for a blanket blessing or even for a blanket condemnation, but rather for a deepening of insight, leading to both thanksgiving and penitence, and to a readiness to be drawn by the Spirit of God along the paths of reconciliation and renewal.

Thus in a theology of the kingdom the Church neither identifies itself with the processes and values of the world nor opposes itself to them. It is neither simply 'for' the world nor simply 'against' it. It is both 'for' and 'against' the world, because it is 'for' God and his rule in and over the world. Moreover, in a theology of this kind Church and world are not totally separate spheres occupied by different sets of persons. Church and world interpenetrate. There is a hidden and anonymous Church in the world wherever and whenever there is a response to the challenges of life with care and love; and the world is to be found in the Church wherever the Church conducts its affairs in the public sphere as one institution among many. Christians, therefore, belong to both Church and world, not in the sense that they think and speak and act differently from Mondays to Fridays from the way in which they think and speak and act on Sundays – although that may be true of them as well – but in the sense that they are all the time subject to two distinct, sometimes overlapping but at other times conflicting, systems of values and sets of principles, both of which are expressions of the way in which God rules his creation.

There is a pressing need to develop at greater depth the complex and dynamic model of kingdom–world–Church and its implications for Christian discipleship and witness. Perhaps, however, enough has already been said to indicate that in a theology of the kingdom the Church's concern cannot be restricted to the ecclesiastical, or even to the religious, if for no other reason than that God's own presence and power are not restricted to the ecclesiastical and the religious. Thus in its discipleship to the kingdom the Church must remain open both God himself and also to God's world. Or, to put the same point in a different way, the Church must always be ready to recognise and respond to God in both his transcendent and his immanent aspects.

This openness both to God and to his world, which in a theology of the kingdom, we have been suggesting, is a special characteristic of the Church, will also be a special characteristic of the Church's ordained ministry, since the ordained ministry is representative of the ministry of the whole Church. (To speak in this way is not to forget that the ministry of the Church is the ministry of Christ in his Church, and that its authority derives first and foremost from the initiative of God, and only secondarily from human response in so far as that response faithfully reflects the mind of God.) We should expect, then, the ordained ministry in some way or other to carry the marks of a divine calling and authorisation, a celebration of the mystery of God's presence in creation, redemption and fulfilment, and a patient service of the needs of the world. In fact these three aspects of ministry, which belong to the whole Church and are focused in the ordained ministry, could be said to find expression in the threefold order of bishop, priest and deacon. It is commonly remarked that bishops, when they are consecrated bishops, despite their change of function, do not thereby cease to be priests and deacons. Might if not also be said that deacons, when they are made deacons, enter upon a ministry which, despite its limited functions, in a sense already participates in the celebratory and authoritative roles of priests and bishops? Service, celebration, authority, although formally and functionally distinguishable, are inseparable in the ministry of the Church.

Thus the ordained minister is a representative sign of the presence in the world of the mystery of God. It is not possible to separate what he does from what he is. Functional and ontological categories are both appropriate. In whatever form he exercises his ministry, he will be a person under authority: he has not chosen Christ, but Christ through his Church has chosen him. The authority which he recognises and in which he therefore participates will be the authority of a servant, of one appointed to serve rather than to be served. It will also be the authority of a witness, making plain in word and sacrament the good news of the gospel and the reality of the divine forgiveness, apart from which there can be no offering of response. In this way he represents Christ in the Church and the Church in Christ. He is a minister of the Church to the Church and on behalf of the Church. He prepares the way for the coming of the kingdom.

With these considerations in mind we can turn now to look at the nature of ordained ministry as exercised in a secular employment.

It must be emphasised at the outset that this is not some different kind of ministry. It will have the same basic character and function as all ministry: it will be the way in which this one ministry finds expression that will be different. Here, then, are some suggestions – and no more than suggestions – how such a ministry might be viewed.

The ordained minister who exercises his ministry at his place of work is an accredited representative of the Church and as such is a sign and symbol of the Church's concern for the world. The world is not rejected by the Church as a god-forsaken place. Rather, God is present in and to the world in judgement and mercy, and so the world has become the place where creation responds to God in obedience and self-offering, so preparing the way for the coming of the kingdom. Thus his presence as an ordained minister of the Church is a sign both of God's promise and also of his judgement. It is a reminder that the world is God's creation. It is also a reminder that the structures of this world are not the ultimate structures of God's kingdom, but only the penultimate structures. In themselves, as we have already suggested, they are ambiguous.

The secular world in which the ordained minister is engaged is and remains secular, and his ordination does not as such equip him with some further secular skill or competence, whether as a teacher, or a counsellor, or something similar. In his secular work secular criteria prevail. If, for example, he is a good teacher, that is because he has learned the skills of teaching, not because of any grace of orders. If, on the other hand, he is a bad teacher, the fact that he is ordained provides him with no excuse. His ordination is, as we have seen, a sign and reminder that the secular is never self-sufficient, since it has its origin, ground and fulfilment in the kingdom of God.

Ordained to be a minister of God's word, the priest in secular employment will find plenty of scope for being an interpreter. Though he himself may 'theologise from above', drawing directly upon the tradition of Christian assumptions, in his reflections and comments in his place of work he is more likely to 'theologise from below', beginning with the human situation as it actually exists, and attempting to dig beneath the surface until its deeper and more ultimate implications become visible. His aim will be to provide stepping-stones between the world and the kingdom. Thus his communication of God's word will as often as not be indirect rather than direct.

His ministry of the sacraments at his place of work will be similarly indirect. Granted that baptism and Holy Communion are the Church's appointed sacraments of the kingdom, other symbolic actions may also express and convey the grace of God and become occasions of celebration, forgiveness and renewal. We may speak, if we wish, of hidden, or secular, sacraments of the kingdom. In these sacraments some ordinary event in life can be revealed as possessing a more than ordinary depth and significance. Thus the ordained minister can often through his secular work exercise a truly sacramental ministry, which is rooted in the two appointed sacraments of the kingdom, but which clothes itself in ordinary secular action and imagery.

His ministry of prayer will also, as likely as not, be a hidden ministry, keeping the boundaries open between kingdom, Church and world, and binding together in spirit what tends to fall apart. It will be a holding operation, a 'gathering' with Christ in the face of those forces which 'scatter', an anticipation of the peace and harmony of the coming kingdom.

In short, in calling an ordained minister who exercises his ministry at his place of work a 'minister of the kingdom', there is no thought of turning him into a loner who separates himself from the life and ministry of the Church. He may be exercising his ministry very much on his own, since he is without the immediate support of those structures of the Church which undergird the parochially based ministry; but he is still a representative of the Church, and he is exercising the same essential ministry which his fellow ministers are exercising in the parishes. What gives its special shape and character to his ministry is the fact that the community to which he belongs, and whose minister he is, is not the geographically based community of the parish gathered round the parish church, but the community of work gathered in the place of work for the purposes of work. It is because he identifies himself with this community of work, and not only with the community of worship of which he may also be a member, that he believes he is being led to exercise his ministry in his place of work. It is for the Church to confirm, authorise and support him in his ministry, if it is to be recognised as truly his 'vocation'.

[1] In K. M. Carey, ed., *The Historic Episcopate* (Dacre Press 1954), p. 17.

[2] W. H. Vanstone, *Love's Endeavour, Love's Expense*, Darton, Longman & Todd 1977.

[3] K. Barth, *Church Dogmatics*, vol. iii pt 3 (T. & T. Clark, Edinburgh 1961), p. 97.

[4] Ibid.

[5] Quoted in D. L. Edwards, *Religion and Change* (Hodder & Stoughton 1969), p. 316.

V   THE PEOPLE OF GOD

The question is often asked: what is the point of being ordained if you intend to exercise your Christian ministry wholly, or almost wholly, at your place of work, especially if more often than not it is going to be 'indirect'? Is not such a ministry something that can be, or ought to be, exercised by any *Christian in virtue of his baptism? This is the question explored by Robin Bennett, who suggests that some at least of the confusion in which we find ourselves is due to the variety of competing models of the Church which have become current among Christians today. His own tentative conclusion is that non-stipendiary ministers may have something of value to give to the Church by way of trail-blazing, but if they take the place of the ministry of the whole people of God then they are leading the Church along a false trail.*

I should like to offer some reflections on the ministry of Christian people that arises ordinarily out of baptism, and to link these thoughts to the development of the various ministries which have been authorised in the last twenty years or so and which include non-stipendiary priests and deaconesses and a range of supportive ministries such as lay pastoral assistants.

'Lay ministry' is commonly used in two senses. One signifies the professional non-stipendiary activity of centrally selected, trained and accredited ministers who are not priests. ACCM has a special committee to support this work. The other signifies the work of the ordinary Christian, which is undertaken without any special selection procedures or examinations.

Not every Christian would think of himself or herself as a minister. The idea has increased in popularity, however, and owes a great deal to a renewed interest in the New Testament Church. Romans 13, for example, speaks about the ministry of the authorities of state, while in 1 Corinthians 12, 1 Peter 1 and Ephesians 4 the differing but complementary gifts of Christians are given special mention and importance. A theology of the Church which emphasises corporateness, based on the images of the body of Christ and the people of God, has been predominant in all the main Churches since 1945. Such a theology teaches that the whole body (or people) is to play an active

41

part in the ministry of the Church, and that this ministry should not be limited only to those who are clergy. Under the influence of these ideas priests and bishops see their role as one of leadership within the body, of enabling the remaining members to exercise their ministry. The idea of ministry itself receives powerful enforcement and comes to occupy a central place in church thinking. Clergy and laity are seen as equal participants in this whole ministry. The word *laos*, often in the past limited to mean those who have not been ordained, now comes to signify the whole people of God, priest included, all working together as a servant Church.

While this insight remains valid, there is nonetheless a need for language which distinguishes roles, which recognises that, within the whole people of God, clergy and laity have different functions. Clergy – and others who exercise a ministry of leadership – give the whole of their time to this work and are paid for it. Indeed, they are paid a stipend so that they may be free from any anxiety about income. Laity, on the other hand, except in a few cases, do not do paid work for the Church, but they fulfil their 'ministry' through their ordinary secular work.

The coming of non-stipendiary ministries has produced people who are in both situations at the same time. No doubt one reason why many transfer to a career in church work is that they have found the pressure of the dual role too severe. Even so, there are a significant number of people who are in this new situation. As far as roles are concerned, however, there has been a general increase – lay, clerical, and now both. Whether this increase is helpful or not, I shall consider later. For the moment I want to stress that, although the majority of those ordained into these new ministries have not remained with their dual role, a large number of them have accepted this duality. This is a new factor in church life, the financial and organisational potential of which has yet to be grasped.

The idea of 'vocation' in the Christian vocabulary has a place in this discussion. The Good Friday collects in both the Book of Common Prayer and the Alternative Service Book speak of 'each in his vocation and ministry', referring to all Christians. Today, however, 'vocation' is commonly used to suggest a call to a priestly life. Indeed, ACCM, which is concerned with offering advice about 'professional' ministries, is the only central agency of the Church of England which employs a 'Vocations Adviser'. Whether the more general use of the word employed by the prayer books could be recaptured is doubtful. This is another reason why the concept of ministry enjoys such popularity, since in our normal usage it has replaced that of vocation. Some excellent lay training programmes have recently been devised with the express intention of encouraging every Christian to consider and pray about the particular 'ministry' to which he or she is called, whether at home or at work or at church. In this context, NSM is but one kind of ministry among many.

There are those, however, who believe that a preoccupation with 'ministry' is not the best way of interpreting the Church today. They fear that it encourages an inward-looking attitude in the Church. This is an important point. God, it is said, as creator and redeemer, is at work in all the world, not just in the Church nor just among its members. God's chosen are chosen in order to be used in his work; they are not chosen for their own sake. God's interest, it follows, is in such matters as the proper sharing of the world's resources, in peace between nations, in education for everyone, in people's social welfare, in the production of wealth, in the government of society, in the physical and mental health of persons and communities, in the creative arts, in laughter and fellowship, in the transformation of suffering. Here is where theology is done. This is where Christian people ought to be, working with God who is already there, as he creates and brings redemption to his universe. Monday's work, Saturday's leisure, Sunday's worship, all contribute to Christian participation in the world. Somehow, ministry is not a sufficient word · for this participation; it offers too limited a view of what Christians are about.

On this view, the role of the Church is to be in the world, both joining in the responsibilities of human beings and keeping alive the rumour of God where it has been forgotten, putting into words and actions the good news of Christ without which, ultimately, the world's affairs are empty. To fulfil such a role often demands courage. It depends on a strong sense of belonging to the Christian community as well as on the sense of authority that comes from such belonging.

Secularism has impressed upon Christians an unhappy division between private faith and public life, such that it feels easier to restrict the remit of faith to one's free time and one's church life, and so it becomes harder to wrestle with the implications of faith for the public world of economics, politics, conflict, cultures and classes, power and wealth. Many are tempted to bow to this pressure and to settle for a private religion only. The quest for inner holiness is an authentic part

43

of the Christian tradition, but it is not the whole of it; and a religion which is only private has colluded with society's wish to avoid the challenge of Christianity. A faith forgotten on Mondays, however sincerely practised it may be on Sundays, is a false religion.

The search for reality in religion can take many forms. One is to accept a role as an accredited representative, a transparently public role. Many candidates for NSM explain their desire for ordination as a wish to have authority. While this authority certainly relates to the task of ministry, it also relates to the *persona* of the minister. He or she takes authority as a person. The Church, the person and society as well all recognise this authority. Those who are 'not recommended' for ordination are often acutely hurt by what seems to them a personal rejection. It is clear that, whatever our theology may say, the experience of some people is that baptism and confirmation do not convey the same sort of authority to be 'real Christians'.

This is a serious matter. Some people at least seem to be saying that there is a loss of confidence in the role of the ordinary Christian. If this is true, then some of our preoccupation with 'ministry' is not in fact about ministry at all, but about the search for authority to live the Christian life.

Behind this suggestion there is a considerable theological confusion. I believe that three different models of the Church are being used for different purposes, and are contributing to this confusion. One is that of the servant Church, from which the idea of ministry takes much of its strength. The second is that of the Church as sacrament, from which so much of the theology of the Ministry takes its content. The third is that of the people of God, which emphasises the participation of all Christians in the work in the Church.[1] The servant Church is modelled after Christ the servant and for inspiration looks to the Servant Songs of Deutero-Isaiah and the synagogue address of Jesus when he inaugurated his ministry. The model of the Church as sacrament owes much to the idea of making our own the experience of faith, so that living the faith, becoming what we truly are, embodying the character of Christ, and having a vision of the Church incarnate in the world are all important aspects of understanding how to live the Christian life. The theology of the people of God stresses the vocation of all who make up that people, their sense of pilgrimage and their separation from other human beings, the mission to which they are called, and the gathered nature of their worship.

A great deal of the theology which values the status of the laity seems to be at odds with the theology which values the special vocation of the clergy. In the past it has sometimes seemed as though the 'real church' consisted of priests and bishops, together with the religious orders, and that anyone not so called belonged to a second class. This view harmonises with the sacramental model, expressing a sort of hierarchy of commitment. A servant theology appears to view all Christian activity as a form of ministry, whereas in history the Church has preferred a number of different images, for example that of the Church militant and missionary, like a mighty army, or that of the Church devotional and spiritual, like a community of worship and prayer. A people of God theology, especially when the model is subtly changed from 'people' to 'family', concentrates on those aspects of church life in which family occasions, family sympathy and support, family worship are viewed as indicative of how Christians should be. All of these models are at present claiming attention in the Church of England. All of them are affecting our understanding of what until recent years was called, on the one hand, the Ministry, and on the other, the work of Christians in general.

It seems to me that this situation is confused theologically. No doubt the confusion owes something to the pressures from the secular world which were mentioned earlier. No doubt, as the numbers and cost of the parochial clergy changed, the Church of England was bound to look for new models. No doubt, too, there have been so many changes in social structures that the one on which the parish system was built is now hopelessly outdated. All this, and perhaps more, is involved. But I want to stress the confusion of theology which is affecting the role of the Christian today, and which, I believe, is prompting some, at least, to doubt their authority as baptised Christians. This is an area in which more work needs to be done.

It is noteworthy that the Methodist Church has resolved not to follow other Churches in having NSMs until it has thought through its model of ministry. The way of the Church of England has been to act first and to let the theology become clear in the process. This method is often used and has much to commend it. I find it important, however, to focus on the confusing aspects of this policy. This confusion can be seen in many parishes, when the different models of Church to which I have referred are commended in turn as incumbents change. Under one leadership, many are encouraged to seek an accredited ministry. Under the next, these ministers find themselves unwanted and unused. Personality clashes are often blamed; perhaps the blame should be on the differences in theologies.

What then of baptism? A great deal of work has been done in parishes to persuade the casual applicant for infant baptism to take it more seriously. Many present-day Christians owe their own commitment to the fact that they were asked to think through their position before they made the promises for a child. There has also been a steady increase in the opportunities given to lay people for learning and education. Much more, no doubt, could be done. But baptism itself does not seem to be held in the same honour it once was. There has been a move towards valuing the experience of faith rather than the givenness of faith. The Catechism has lost its former prominence. One rarely hears sermons about God's initiative, or the status of baptism; it is far more often the human response that is spoken about, as though baptism were not itself a real event. Perhaps this is why some laity are seeking further authorisation through accreditation and why so many are joining training courses. Perhaps they are seeking new confidence. Several speak of being asked to seek ordination although they feel no sense of personal vocation for it. It seems to me that the Church of England is showing signs of losing confidence in the role of the ordinary Christian, and of wishing to place too much stress on ministry, whereas it is baptism that is the sacramental incorporation of a person into Christ, the sign of his authority to live the Christian life, the life of a forgiven sinner.

I would, then, make a plea that we should take seriously the role of the baptised Christian people, viewing Sunday's worship as an occasion when they are sustained in their dependence upon God and prepared for their service during the week. This is the fundamental 'ministry' or 'liturgy' of the Christian people. In so far as non-stipendiary ministers are those who 'go before' the Christian, as a sign and a forerunner of the Christian people, they are doing a valuable job. In as far as they are acting in place of the Christian lay person, they are causing confusion and making it harder for others to accept authority for their own fundamental ministry as God's people.

---

[1] These models are derived from Avery Dulles, s.j., *Models of the Church*, Gill-Macmillan 1976.

VI CALLING AND COMMUNITY

One of the questions which arises in connection with the idea of 'vocation' is the question what it is to which a Christian may be 'called'. Is it to discipleship in the kingdom of God? Is it to membership of the Church? Is it to ministry? And if it is to ministry, is this the ordained ministry, or may some secular 'job of work' itself be a form of Christian ministry? However, there are other equally fundamental questions connected with 'vocation' which call for consideration. For example, who is it that does the 'calling'? Is it God? Is it the Church? Or, perhaps, God through the Church? And again, how is 'vocation' recognised? In a brief historical excursus Kenneth Noakes distinguishes between the ideas of 'vocation' and 'choice', argues that much Anglican thought has been over-individualistic, and suggests that that form of non-stipendiary ministry which is indigenous and centred on a parish may help us to rediscover the 'older understanding of vocation in which call and choice are seen to be one'. If Noakes is right in seeking to redress the balance between the individual and the community, this has something of importance to suggest concerning non-stipendiary ministry in the place of work as well as in the parish. The non-stipendiary minister in a place of work must have an authority recognised by the community which both 'calls' and 'sends' him into this ministry. Practically speaking, he must have the encouragement and support of the Church. But if he is to be the Church's minister in a place of work, he needs also to have his authority recognised by the community of work. This double 'recognition' may well provide the rationale for an ordained ministry at a place of work, something which need not be totally different from the incidental ministry of the baptised Christian, but which nevertheless focuses and expresses the Church's ministry in a distinctive and authoritative way.

In Anglican tradition there has been an inordinate stress on the sense of 'inward call' as a necessary prerequisite for ordination. H. L. Goudge commented:

> The first question put to those to be ordained to the Diaconate in the Anglican Ordinal – 'Do you trust that you are inwardly called by the Holy Ghost to take upon you this office and ministration . . .?' – is nothing less than a disaster. It has probably lost to the ministry hundreds of men who might have made admirable clergy; and it tends to cause painful searchings of heart in times of depression to many rightly ordained. A good

47

meaning can be attached to the question, but what it suggests is the necessity for a strong sense of vocation, as in the case of an Old Testament prophet.

This question about inward call appears in the Ordinal because

> Our Reformers, misled by Martin Bucer, confused the regular with the prophetic ministry. The position of prophets does largely rest upon their inward call. The Church . . . recognises their position and discriminates between true prophecy and false; but it does no more than this. But the position of the regular ministers, who may have no remarkable gifts, depends upon their ordination and commission by the Apostles, and it is for others to judge of their suitability rather than for themselves. They must believe that they are doing the will of God in what they do, and must keep back nothing which those who ordain ought to know; but Scripture does not justify us in asking more than this, nor does any Church Ordinal earlier than the sixteenth century.[1]

In Anglican practice vocation has often been understood in terms of a contract between God and the man who feels himself called. The vocation is certainly a call to serve the Church, but the vocation is not mediated by the Church; it is a matter between God and an individual. The Church's part is to 'test' vocations, to examine a man's subjective sense of vocation to determine whether it is genuine. There is an element of caricature, perhaps, in the above description, but it cannot be denied that vocation has often been disastrously misunderstood as something essentially private, individualistic, unmediated, the result of direct contact between God and the person concerned. The ecclesial dimension of vocation has been seriously neglected. Because of this neglect there has been a disjunction between 'call' and 'choice'. A person claims to have experienced a call and the Church subsequently exercises a choice, deciding whether that man should be ordained or not.

The development of the non-stipendiary priesthood, a form of indigenous priesthood, can lead to a rediscovery of the part played by the local church in calling suitable candidates to the priesthood. A local Christian community, aware of its needs and resources, can be the mediator of a call to someone within that community. The gap between call and choice is bridged.

It may be observed that despite a generally individualistic understanding of vocation, the ecclesial dimensions have not been entirely obscured – in well-ordered parishes vocations have been assiduously fostered and ordinands carefully nurtured. However, until the development of the non-stipendiary priesthood, vocations were fostered for elsewhere and ordinands were nurtured to serve elsewhere. The local church community was not able to assess its own needs and resources and be the agent of call and place of nurture for its own priests.

The topics of call and choice, as well as other aspects of ministry, have been illuminated by the recent work of Fr E. Schillebeeckx, OP.[2] He has drawn a sharp contrast between the concept of the ministry which prevailed in the first ten centuries and that which has prevailed in the second Christian millennium. In the former period there is a 'pneumatological and ecclesial conception of the ministry'. The concept of ordination includes not only a bishop's laying on of hands together with *epiclesis,* or prayer to the Holy Spirit, but also, and primarily, being called and appointed by a definite Christian community. 'The community calls and this is the calling or vocation of the priest, but, because the community regards itself as a "community of Jesus" the ecclesial appointment is at the same time experienced as a "gift of the Holy Spirit", in other words as a pneumatological event.'[3]

The second millennium is associated with a fading of the notion of the Church into the background and an increasingly private understanding of ministry. In this period

A man has or feels that he has a vocation to the priesthood. He makes an application (this shows that the ecclesial bond has not been completely lost) and is trained for the priesthood and finally ordained. Everything is settled and he only has to wait to know where the bishop will send him. Ordination continues to be an accreditation of the priest as an office-bearer to a diocesan region, it is true, but the concrete place or community to which he will be sent remains open. What has completely disappeared in this procedure is the call of the community, which was in the early Church the essential element of ordination.[4]

Schillebeeckx draws out the contrast between the first and second millennia by pointing out the difference between the regulations of the Council of Chalcedon (451) and those of the Third Lateran Council (1179). Canon 6 of Chalcedon expresses an ecclesial view of ministry, forbidding 'absolute ordinations', i.e. ordinations of candidates without any connection with a particular community, and declaring them to be invalid: 'No one, neither priest nor deacon, may be ordained in an absolute manner . . . if he has not been clearly assigned to a local community, either in the city or in the country, either in a martyrium [burial place where a martyr is venerated] or in a monasterium.' 'The Sacred Council concludes that their ordination is null and void . . . and that they may not carry out any functions on any occasion.' Therefore, only someone called by a definite community to be its leader may receive ordination.

The Third Lateran Council reflects the rise of feudalism; the *Titulus Ecclesiae*, on the basis of which men were ordained according to Chalcedon, is radically reduced to the purely feudal matter of a benefice: no one may be ordained 'unless he has been assured of a reasonable livelihood.' As well as the rise of feudalism, the renaissance of Roman law had a powerful effect on the understanding of the ordained ministry.

Interpreted juridically, the priest is a man who possesses sacred power (*sacra potestas*). By virtue of his ordination he has all priestly power in his own person. Specifically, he has the power to perform the consecration in the Eucharist. A distinction is now made between the power of ordination and the power of jurisdiction. Although the ordained man might not be assigned a Christian community (i.e. legally speaking has no *potestas jurisdictionis*), by virtue of ordination he still has all priestly power in his own person. So the link between ministry and a particular Christian community is weakened, if not broken altogether. Priesthood is seen as a personal state of life, a 'status', rather than as a service to the community; it has been individualised and made something private.

Anglican practice, with its stress on 'inward call', has reflected this individualised view of ministry in which the call of the community has disappeared. If we turn back to the first millennium of the Church's life to learn something of vocation, the nature of call and choice in respect of the ordained ministry, so that the past can confront the present constructively for the sake of the future, we shall doubtless be accused of 'patristic fundamentalism'. However, as Schillebeeckx has shown, this charge is wide of the mark if we are concerned with the theology of ministry, for in the first millennium the Church's practice with regard to office was primarily formed on the basis of theological criteria (although in a definite historical setting), whereas in the second millennium radical changes occurred largely on the basis of non-theological factors.

Perhaps the development of indigenous non-stipendiary priesthood can help us rediscover this older understanding of vocation in which call and choice are seen to be one. Two practical caveats need to be

Calling and Community

registered. First, the local Christian community needs to be made aware of itself as a unit of the wider Church. In putting forward suitable men for the ordained ministry the local Christian unit cannot act autonomously but must be guided by the bishop and his advisers, who may well have deeper insights into the real needs of a community than those who live within it. A local church can easily be mistaken about itself: what it wants is not always what it needs. Secondly, the local community needs to be made aware of the specific nature of Christian leadership, which always bears the marks of humble service and not of domination. Success in a particular career, or experience of the world, may not be very relevant to the true exercise of priesthood within the Church. The man with 'natural' leadership qualities, who, for example, is obviously a good organiser of others, may not necessarily be the person who should be put forward by the local community for the ordained ministry. In this sphere of vocation, as in every other, the Church must seek not to be conformed to this world but to discover the mind of Christ.

[1] H. L. Goudge, *The Church of England and Reunion* (1938), p. 181.
[2] See E. Schillebeeckx, 'The Christian Community and its Office Bearers', in E. Schillebeeckx and J. B. Metz, 'Right of the Community to a Priest', *Concilium*, no. 133, 1980, pp. 95–133, and E. Schillebeeckx, *Ministry: A Case for Change*, 1981.
[3] *Concilium*, loc. cit., p. 102.
[4] *Concilium*, loc. cit., p. 111.

VII WORD AND SACRAMENT

According to the Book of Common Prayer a priest is given authority to preach the word of God and to administer the sacraments. It has already been suggested that the communication of the gospel may be indirect as well as direct, and that there are implicit as well as explicit sacraments which a priest may celebrate. In the first section of this chapter Ian Cundy develops this line of thought with regard to the ministry of the word, while in the second section Kenneth Noakes develops it with regard to the ministry of the sacrament.

(1) Ministry of the Word

CONTEXT

Among the significant contributions to the debates of the General Synod on the Partners in Mission report *To a Rebellious House?* were those of the Provost of Southwark (David Edwards) and the then Bishop of Durham (John Habgood). The former pointed out that the PIM assessors had failed to appreciate the extent of secularisation in Britain and described our problem as 'the loss of the sense of God'. The malaise in evangelism was therefore as much a failure to speak of God in a *relevant* way – to convince a secular society 'that God is real and alive and eternal' – as an act of unfaithfulness on the Church's part. The bishop, with a theme he has developed in *Church and Nation in a Secular Age,*[1] described 'the loss of a whole cultural dimension which enables people to feel that religion in whatever form is an important activity'. In a pluralist society religion can become little more than 'one among a number of leisure-time activities'.[2] Our understanding of the ministry of the word needs to take that present context seriously and to be conducted in ways which effectively engage with modern society. In particular it needs to demonstrate that Christianity is not merely 'a leisure-time activity' for some but a faith which pervades and enhances all human activity – personal and social.

There is an imbalance in writing about the ordained ministry which has interpreted the primary context of the ministry of the word as that of the community gathered for worship. Even Max Thurian, who recognises that ministry is conditioned by the social and political context of its time, writes:

Demands born of the secularisation of the modern world are forcing the Church to rethink the presbyterate in its sociological context ... It is certainly too early to know how the basic Christian Ministry will find expression in modern society without losing any of its originality, while adapting itself to man's condition today. Above all, it is important to distinguish what is specific to the presbyteral ministry, to do some healthy demythologizing to rediscover it in its fundamental intention, in its permanent meaning across the accidents of history. And here we must dwell more particularly on its priestly and sacrificial nature.[3]

This he expounds in terms of the priesthood of mission, the office of intercession and the presidency of the eucharist. It is an admirable exposition with many stimulating biblical insights. But the question must be asked whether the socio-religious situation which informs it is that of the ecumenical endeavour, with its desire to bring together traditional 'protestant' emphases – 'the minister is firstly a man of God's word, of the Bible, of the truth revealed and lived in the Church'[4] – and 'catholic' ones – the Eucharist 'is at the very heart of the presbyteral ministry' – rather than that of the secular world which needs to 'hear' the gospel with increasing clarity. It is surprising that in a contemporary study of the ordained ministry the concept of non-stipendiary ministry receives only a passing reference in the postscript, which merely affirms its validity.

Those writers who have explored the theology of NSM in relation to their work situation, on the other hand, have tended to concentrate on a sacramental and ontological understanding of ministry and to develop the concept of a recognised (and recognisable) 'Christian presence' in the world. But the ministry of word and sacrament belong together: 'the word needs the concreteness and breadth of the sacraments: while the sacraments need the conceptual and intelligible structure of of the word. Where one too much overshadows the other, the results have always been unfortunate'.[5]

Max Thurian's work, for all its helpful insights, still views the minister's primary work in relation to the Christian community: building up the body of Christ so that 'they' – the laity – may work effectively (and missiologically?) in the world. The challenge voiced by Patrick Vaughan in the light pf of his research has not been taken up: 'the attempt must be made to discuss the Christian understanding of ministry and ordination in a manner that is informed amongst other things by the praxis of NSM...and is not dominated by parochial models of thinking'.[6] On the other hand the model of ministry which expounds the concept of the worker-priest as a 'priest for mankind or creation' largely ignores the Christian community. The pendulum has swung in the other direction.

The biblical concept of service relates both to the world and to others in the community. Ministry is *apostolic,* sent into the world; *prophetic,* declaring God's truth; *pastoral* and *didactic,* building up the community. The context of Christian ministry is both the secular world and the worshipping body of Christ. This is not only true to the 'givenness' of the faith but also to the 'praxis' of NSM, as Patrick Vaughan has indicated.

THE MINISTRY OF THE WORD

It is obvious that the ministry of the word involves more than preaching sermons. Nevertheless the Anglican Church has always tended to take as its norm for understanding ordained ministry the model of a sole incumbent in a parish. The result is that, in spite of our declared beliefs, our theology of ministry has a largely unconscious sociological bias (if not an ecclesiological one) towards a gathered pietist church. So we interpret the apostolic injunction 'preach the word, be urgent, in season and out of season, convince, rebuke and exhort...' (2 Tim. 4.2) entirely in terms of the opportunities afforded by the pulpit and the pastoral visit.

A study of modern ecumenical texts, however, reveals a growing theological consensus that the ministry of the ordained person must be set and understood in the light of the ministry of the *laos* – the whole Church of God – and not vice versa. It is, as John Tiller pointed out, an awkward moment for producing a working definition of orders in the Church of England.[7] The consensus of Lima[8] and ARCIC,[9] however, would suggest that there is growing acceptance of the view that the early Church was making a significant theological statement in building on the developing concept of order in the New Testament and isolating a threefold ministry as 'a representative focus of *the Church's authority* to minister the Gospel in Christ's name.'[10] With a similar insight, Jürgen Moltmann isolates a fourfold charge to the Christian community of proclaiming the gospel, baptizing and celebrating the Lord's Supper, assembling together and carrying out charitable work, and suggests that *kerygma, koinonia* and *diakonia* are essential for the community. They therefore need preachers, presbyters and deacons as representatives of the Church's mission and enablers of the whole people of God.[11]

In spite of such a theology, Lima appears to revert to a parochial model in saying that 'the chief responsibility of the ordained ministry is to assemble and build up the body of Christ by proclaiming and teaching the Word of God, by celebrating the sacraments, and by guiding the life of the community in its worship, its mission and its caring ministry.'[12] That suggests an inadequate and limited 'representative focus' of the Church's ministry for a number of reasons, which apply to the work of the ordained ministry in general as well as to their ministry of the word in particular:

First, they must be truly representative of the totality of the Church's mission – both its evangelism and its social action, both the individuality and the corporate nature of its message. Secondly, the majority of Christians (the *laos*) do not 'work out their salvation' in an ecclesiastical context. Most of their time and much of their energy is spent in occupations of a different kind, in which the significance of Christ has to be discerned. They may want to point to the Church as a paradigm of his kingdom; but if the ministry of the word has nothing to say in and to their daily lives in a secular society than their faith has become the leisure activity of which John Habgood warned. Thirdly, at the heart of the gospel lie the incarnation and the cross – symbols of sacrificial involvement and identity with the ills of humanity. Together they speak of God's affirmation of the world as well as his judgement and rebuke. It was God's love of the world that provided the motivation for the mission of his Son; it is the world that he died to redeem, and his disciples are 'in the world, though not of the world'. The ministry of the word must therefore wrestle with the significance of Christ in a way which is world-affirming and not world-denying.

If we accept this idea that the ordained and 'recognised' ministry reflects and focuses the ministry of the laity – the total people of God – and therefore the essence of the gospel, we can develop an understanding of this ministry in terms of a number of gospel motifs. Ruth Etchells[13] has highlighted two of these motifs: the paradoxes of 'the hidden work of God, the secret power of the kingdom, set against the openness of proclamation of God at work on earth', and of 'a servant Church' expressing 'an authority and power which goes far beyond that of the earthly'. She argues that

> The character and distinctiveness of the *laos* of God is in some way concerned with both aspects of the Church's nature: as *both* the visible

55

expression in the world of the kingdom of God, *and* of the hiddenness of the work of God; as both authoritative (not authoritarian) *and* serving. Much of our difficulty, however, has arisen from allowing a corruption of these paradoxes to take control: of confusing the visible with the strident, and the hidden with the non-operative; or the authoritative with the power-hungry, and the serving with the servile.

The Church, as the *laos* of God, must display the visibility of the city set on a hill and the light which fills a room as well as the hiddenness of salt, of the mustard seed and of the pearl of great price.

Furthermore, its 'recognition' of certain ministries must testify to both the authority of the Church – 'I have overcome the world' (John 16.33); 'This is the victory that overcomes the world, our faith' (1 John 5.4) – and its servant quality – 'I am among you as he who serves'. So the ministers of the word may speak to the world with the authority of Christ, but they also need to adopt a servant role; their attitude to and engagement with the world say as much as, and often more than, the content of their pronouncements.

A third motif reflects the individual and corporate nature of the gospel. We are incorporated into Christ (as individuals) and into the community of believers. Our models of ministry need to reflect that tension. We are today increasingly recognising that the ordained ministry contains people of widely differing gifts and that their representative functions may need to be carried out corporately, often in terms of teams or groups. There is ample precedent for this in the New Testament, where elders rarely if ever worked on their own. Within such a team structure it is possible to develop different kinds of ministry, where the ordained ministry is both encouraging and strengthening the community and also working at the frontiers of the Church's mission in terms of the challenges and questions raised by being Christian in our secularised society.

NON-STIPENDIARY MINISTRY

Much of the early theology relating to the non-stipendiary ministry, from Roland Allen onwards, has expounded their ministry primarily in terms of the parochial model. Thus Allen viewed them as 'voluntary clergy' and sought the ordination of 'men who earn their living by the work of their hands or their heads in the common market and serve as clergy without stipend or fee of any kind'.[14] He regarded secular work as 'tentmaking', following the example of Paul. Such a view dominated the English discussions well into the 1960s. A. M. Ramsey, however, writing in 1972, commented: 'I regard the contemporary development of a priesthood which combines a ministry of word and sacrament with employment in a secular profession not as a modern fad but as a recovery of something indubitably apostolic and primitive . . . and we may learn from them of that inward meaning of priesthood which we share with him.'[15] And in 1980 Anthony Russell suggested that the non-stipendiary ministry could be a 'means towards opening up a new understanding of the way in which the Church's ministry may be performed in the much altered social conditions of the last quarter of the twentieth century'.[16]

In between Roland Allen and these later writers, a separate strand of thinking had emerged with its origin in the French concept of a 'worker priest'. It was expounded by Mervyn Stockwood as the basis for the founding of the Southwark Ordination Course. It saw the primary role of the non-stipendiary minister in terms of his employment rather than his parish and stressed the ontological – 'being' – aspect of his ministry, while Allen had tended to emphasise the functional.[17] Patrick Vaughan has suggested that most NSMs today work happily with *both* these models and that to try to hold them apart theologically does not do justice to current experience. He also points out that 'preaching does not require a pulpit'.[18] All this is consistent with a theology of the laity and of ministry which takes seriously the tensions of the gospel which we have expounded.

Four particular aspects of this ministry have wide significance for the Church:
1 Their ministry affirms that of the whole people of God. There has always been a tendency to interpret lay ministry in terms of clerical. Too many people today see the role of the laity in terms of making more 'clergy people' and involving them in leadership of services, church committees and the like. NSM points to a different understanding, both in terms of enabling all to minister (cf. Ephesians 4) and also in terms of the ordained ministry focusing the ministry of the community. Some of the early opposition to the concept of an auxiliary ministry was voiced in terms of a fear that it would 'de-skill' the laity and that ordained men and women in full-time non-ecclesiastical employment would prevent the laity fulfilling their Christian mission. Patrick Vaughan's research has suggested that the reality is precisely the reverse.[19] By their very existence they are saying

57

something about the nature of Christian ministry and the truth of the gospel. As such it is a silent ministry of the word but no less deafening for that.

2 Patrick Vaughan has also exposed the frequency with which non-stipendiary ministers view their role as that of interpreter of the Church to the world and of the world to the Church. In view of the problems to which we referred at the beginning of this essay, both the failure of the Church to speak realistically about God and also the difficulty of finding appropriate models today through which to express the concept of the transcendent, this is clearly vital and important. There is a danger that professional clergy and professional theologians talk only to each other and to those who work with their models. However much we try to avoid that danger by contact outside the ecclesiastical world, we rarely have the perception of someone who is, by virtue of employment, thoroughly immersed in modern society.

This particular role has an important contribution in the life of the worshipping community and in terms of the Church's mission. In the former it was a contribution which Roland Allen anticipated. In referring to the preaching of his proposed voluntary clergy, which others apparently suspected would be deficient in theology and learning, he remarked:

> The sermons might not indeed be the type of theological sermon with which we are familiar but they would be extremely practical and closely related to the life of the little community from which they sprang. They would be far more intelligible to their hearers than many of the sermons preached by the clergy trained in theological schools.[20]

NSMs are uniquely qualified to expound the relevance of the Christian truth in our contemporary world. As such, they may well not be a welcome or comforting occupant of the pulpit, but they are essential to the true ministry of the word. Other ministers are trained to be good at biblical exegesis or at distilling the current theological thinking into more or less manageable form, but we are weakest on the *praxis* of daily living in a secular age. Others have pointed out the necessity and value of expounding our theology in 'secular' terms – for example Michael Ranken, in a stimulating article,[21] explains what it means for him and his fellow NSMs 'to tell the world that the church's vision of God is true'. In doing so he takes a number of situations in which they have been involved and interprets them theologically. He demonstrates how often the truth of our symbols is visible in the reality of the world. The gospel, he argues, can be validly discussed entirely in the terminology of the 'out-there world' but so often 'we prefer the symbols to the reality'. The Dean of Durham made a similar point at a recent conference for NSMs. 'The only way to engagement with unbelievers and sceptics is to do your theology from their side – providing stepping-stones, so that they can step towards faith . . . so to live that one's life would be inexplicable if God did not exist.'

3 The Christian Church has always had a role as a prophet to the world. Its task is to declare God's word as it applies to given and specific situations. Part of that declaration will often involve a word of judgement as well as a word of hope. In the early Church the ministry of the prophet, who focused the Church's work in this area in his own person, seems to have been valued almost as highly as that of the apostles. There is evidence from the Didache and other early writings that some tension existed between the emerging settled ministries of presbyter and deacon and the itinerant ministries of the apostle and the prophet.

It is obvious that, if it is to be of any use, prophecy needs to be heard by those to whom God's words are addressed. In terms of our modern society, bishops in the House of Lords, the writers of books, local clergy who have earned the right to be heard in their local council chamber, have a prophetic voice, as do many others. There remains, however, a unique and important contribution which the NSM is uniquely qualified to execute and in so doing to focus the prophetic ministry of the Church. He or she is, by virtue of employment, in constant touch with the secular world and can bring together an intimate knowledge of society and an understanding of Christian truth and its significance.

4 Their ministry expresses the hiddenness of the kingdom. All Christians are those who through their response to Jesus Christ have entered the kingdom – they have acknowledged and recognised his rule and his authority. Thereafter their lives need to reflect the standards and aspirations of the kingdom of God. Actions speak louder than words, and clearly the life that speaks through its attitudes and behaviour is as much part of the ministry of the word as all the things that issue from our mouth in terms of formal sermons and teaching. In his embodiment of the kingdom the full-time professional ordained priest could suggest that the kingdom is detached from the world, masculine and exclusive. Positively, his

59

separation from other employment may bear witness to the points of discontinuity between the world and the kingdom. The paradox of the kingdom, however, includes its hiddenness and the elements of continuity with the world as well. It is these latter aspects that are focused and demonstrated by the embodiment of the kingdom in the life of a non-stipendiary minister. He or she expresses more acutely and realistically than the stipendiary minister the hiddenness of the kingdom within their life and the visibility of carrying the accreditation and the recognition of the Church. To quote Ruth Etchells again:

> The more hidden the co-partnership of the laity with their Lord in proclaiming the day of liberation, the more of a challenge that *laos* can be to the shape of the 'recognised' ministry. In reverse, of course, the greater (is) the duty of the visibly recognised to seek the 'hidden' richness of the *laos*.

It is in such ways as these that the advent of non-stipendiary ministry has raised questions relating both to the style and to the nature of ministry today. Underlying them all is a vision of the Church as an open rather than a closed society – a Church which is open to God, to the future and to the world. If the Church is simply a closed society which lives for its own aggrandisement, then clearly ministry merely relates to its upbuilding. But mission is an important strand in the New Testament teaching about the Church – a mission of which Jesus is the pattern (cf. John 17). If the advent of non-stipendiary ministry has made us ask questions about our openness to the world and the parochialism of our ministry then it has served as a valuable catalyst. In that sense it has been a 'means towards opening up a new understanding of the way in which the Church's ministry may be performed in the much-altered social conditions of the last quarter of the twentieth century'.

---

[1] J. Habgood, *Church and Nation in a Secular Age*, Darton, Longman & Todd 1983.
[2] General Synod, *Report of Proceedings*, November 1982.
[3] M. Thurian, *Priesthood and Ministry: Ecumenical Research* (Mowbray 1983), p. 111.
[4] Ibid., p. 119.
[5] J. Macquarrie, *Principles of Christian Theology* (SCM Press, 1st edn 1966), p. 399.
[6] P. Vaughan, *How Do Non-Stipendiary Ministers Perceive the Nature of their Ministry in the World of Work?*, a Research Project prepared for the Mid Service Clergy Course XXVIII (July 1983) at St George's House, Windsor Castle, p. 31.
[7] J. Tiller, *A Strategy for the Church's Ministry* (CIO 1983), p. 83.
[8] *Baptism, Eucharist and Ministry*, Faith and Order Paper no. 11, WCC 1982.

9 Anglican-Roman Catholic International Commission, *The Final Report*, CTS/SPCK 1982.
10 Tiller, op. cit., p. 84 (my italics).
11 J. Moltmann, *The Church in the Power of the Spirit* (SCM Press 1977), p. 306.
12 Op. cit., p. 22.
13 In an unpublished paper on the theology of the laity. Ruth Etchells is the Principal of St John's College, Durham.
14 In D. Paton, ed., *The Ministry of the Spirit: Selected Writings of Roland Allen* (Lutterworth Press 1960), p. 147.
15 A. M. Ramsey, *The Christian Priest Today* (SPCK) 1972, p. 4.
16 A. Russell, *The Clerical Profession* (SPCK 1980), p. 382.
17 See P. Vaughan, 'Historical Background', in M. Hodge, *Non-Stipendiary Ministry in the Church of England* (GS 583A: CIO 1983), pp. 9–24.
18 Vaughan, *How Do Non-Stipendiary Ministers...*, p. 27.
19 See chapter III above.
20 Paton, op. cit., p. 176.
21 M. Ranken, 'A Theology for the Priest at Work', *Theology*, vol. LXXXV, March 1982, pp. 108–13.

(2) Ministry of the Sacrament

In the ARCIC documents and the Lima text[1] there is a recognition that 'priesthood' is a term used in a threefold way in Christian discourse. First, it is used of the unique priesthood of Christ. Secondly, it is used of the priesthood of the whole people of God. Thirdly, it is used of the priesthood of the ordained ministry. These second and third usages are derivatives, depending on the first. The priesthood of the whole people of God is the consequence of incorporation by baptism into Christ. 'All members are called to offer their being "as a living sacrifice" and to intercede for the Church and the salvation of the world'.[2] The Lima text speaks of the priesthood of the ordained ministry in functional terms: 'they may appropriately be called priests because they fulfil a particular priestly service by strengthening and building up the loyal and prophetic priesthood of the faithful through word and sacraments, through their prayers of intercession and through their pastoral guidance of the community.' ARCIC goes beyond this functional approach, saying that 'their ministry is not an extension of the common Christian priesthood but belongs to another realm of the gifts of the Spirit',[3] that the ordained ministry is called priestly principally because it has a particular sacramental relationship with Christ as High Priest.

Although we have argued for the recognition of the essential role of

61

the Church in the call of a person to the priesthood,[4] it is important to emphasise that priesthood is not delegated from the Church to an individual but is, rather, a divine gift for the sake of the whole Church. While the relationship between the two is not one of delegation from one to the other but rather of sharing a common source, the priesthood of the whole people of God and the priesthood of the ordained ministry cannot be dissociated (cf. Chalcedon's ban on absolute ordinations). The Lima text speaks helpfully of this interrelationship:

> All members of the believing community, ordained and lay, are interrelated. On the one hand, the community needs ordained ministers. Their presence reminds the community of the divine initiative, and of the dependence of the Church on Jesus Christ, who is the source of its mission and the foundation of its unity. They serve to build up the community in Christ and to strengthen its witness. In them the Church seeks an example of holiness and loving concern. On the other hand, the ordained ministry has no existence apart from the community. Ordained ministers can fulfil their calling only in and for the community. They cannot dispense with the recognition, the support and the encouragement of the community.[5]

Christian priesthood is not to be defined in exclusively cultic terms. Nevertheless, it is in the Eucharist that the priesthood of the Church and the priesthood of the ordained ministry within it are made most explicit. When the Eucharist is celebrated the Church associates herself with Christ's priestly self-giving and the Church's offering of herself is caught up into Christ's one sufficient offering.

In his classic study R. C. Moberly emphasises the representative character of such priesthood. This representation is specially evident in the celebration of the Eucharist:

> the Christian ministry is not a substituted intermediary – still less an atoning mediator – between God and lay people; but it is rather the representative and organ of the whole body, in the exercise of prerogatives and powers which belong to the body as a whole. It is ministerially empowered to wield, as the body's organic representative, the powers which belong to the *body*, but which the body cannot wield except through its own organs duly fitted for the purpose. What is duly done by Christian Ministers, it is not so much that *they* do it, in the stead, or for the sake, of the whole; but rather that the whole does it by and through them. The Christian Priest does not offer an atoning sacrifice on behalf of the Church; it is rather the Church through his act that, not so much 'offers an atonement', as 'is identified upon earth with the one heavenly offering of the atonement of Christ'.[6]

The ARCIC statement on Ministry and Ordination takes up this theme of representation; Christian ministers 'are – particularly in presiding at the eucharist – representative of the whole Church in the fulfilment of its priestly vocation of self-offering to God as a living sacrifice (Rom. 12.1).[7] There is a double representation in that not only does the ordained minister represent the priesthood of the whole people of God but also he is a symbol of Christ within the eucharistic assembly. This latter theme is stressed in the Lima text:

> It is especially in the eucharistic celebration that the ordained ministry is the visible focus of the deep and all-embracing communion between Christ and the members of his body. In the celebration of the eucharist Christ gathers, teachers and nourishes the Church. It is Christ who invites to the meal and who presides at it. In most churches this presidency is signified and represented by an ordained minister.[8]

Richard Hanson sees this double representation, of God to men and of men to God, as characteristic of true priesthood. He writes of this representation at the Eucharist:

> But though the Christian priest must not be defined by the cult, it is altogether fitting that he should be the main minister in conducting the cult. When he celebrates the eucharist the priest is acting for men to God and for God to men most representatively, most fully, most appropriately. The fact that his status is not defined by the cult need not lead him to undervalue either the cult or his part in it. He is, after all, as he celebrates, the concentration of the priesthood of Christ's people who leads them into their priesthood, not fulfilling it instead of them, as their substitute, but as their representative and spokesman and leader. And he has, by ordination, the authority of the Church, the authority of Christ acting and ordaining in the Church, not only to represent them to God but also to speak to them on God's behalf, in God's name. Even though he is not the only person to speak and act in God's name, still he bears that authority.[9]

That in the Eucharist the priest is more than the people's representative is made clear by Michael Ramsey in an address entitled 'Why the Priest?' He describes the priest as the man of theology and prayer, as minister of reconciliation and the man of the Eucharist. With regard to the latter role he writes:

> As celebrant he is more than the people's representative. In taking, breaking and consecrating he acts in Christ's name and in the name not only of the particular congregation but of the Holy Catholic Church down the ages. By his Office as celebrant he symbolizes the focusing of the

Eucharist in the givenness of the historic gospel and in the continuing life of the Church as rooted in that gospel.[10]

We may accept that the priesthood of the whole Church and the priesthood of the ordained ministry within it find their most explicit expression when the Eucharist is celebrated. But what does this have to do with stipendiary or non-stipendiary forms of ministry? A priest is a priest, whatever the source of his income. This is true, but we may perhaps learn something of value by attending to the role of the non-stipendiary priest as the man of the Eucharist.

It is to the contrast between explicit and implicit priesthood that I wish to direct attention. For any priest, the Eucharist provides the focus, the heart of his ministry. It is in the Eucharist that his priesthood within the priesthood of the whole Church becomes most explicit. A stipendiary priest may well find that much of his time is spent on tasks which are not specifically priestly, often tasks of administration and management of people and resources. Yet his priesthood is always potentially explicit; he is free from the commitment of 'work' so that he is available for the tasks which relate more closely to priesthood, tasks such as teaching the Faith, intercessory prayer, giving spiritual direction, administering the sacraments. For good or ill, the stipendiary priest is seen as a member of a clerical profession. People have certain expectations of him, and some of these expectations relate to the sphere of explicit priesthood.

By contrast, the non-stipendiary priest, who is not seen as a professional clergyman, may find that a large proportion of his priesthood remains at the implicit level. An overt priestly ministry may not be sought, or may be quite impossible at his place of work; he may work alone for much of the time, or the environment may be hostile to any explicit expression of priesthood, or loyalty to the employer who pays him may inhibit such expression. Priesthood which is not overt is none the less, in its hiddenness, a real sharing in Christ's priesthood and his prayer of self-offering. Freedom from the constraints of the traditional expectations attaching to the professional clergyman may encourage the development of authentic modes of priesthood in the most diverse circumstances. However, the difficulty in coping with a largely implicit ministry is probably a major reason for the drift from non-stipendiary to stipendiary ministry.

For those whose ministry is largely implicit, the Eucharist will be of vital importance as the place where priesthood is made explicit. Michael Ranken wrote of this:

A few of us may have altars, or maybe portable Tents of Presence, in our work places where the Church's worship and sacraments may be ministered in something like the ordinary way. Most of us are likely instead to ask the high privilege of exercising the ministry on behalf of our work, in our parish churches. Like the Hebrew priests, we enter the sanctuary alone or with our brother priests. Few or none of those whose work we share will be nearby, yet we offer all of the sacrifices which they have brought before us, in the one cup, on their behalf and on the world's. And thereby we too, and the Church, are miraculously strengthened.[11]

The movement from implicit to explicit ministry and back again, from the world of work to the Eucharist and back again, is something shared by non-stipendiary priests and lay people. Stipendiary priests, with their status of 'professional clergymen', know less of this oscillation from their own experience. It may be an important task for a non-stipendiary priest to help his fellow Christians to integrate their experience, as he seeks by God's grace to integrate his own experience, so that liturgy and life interact creatively.

[1] References are to the section 'Ministry and Ordination' and its Elucidation in ARCIC, *The Final Report* (CTS/SPCK 1982), pp. 29–45, and to the section 'Ministry' in *Baptism, Eucharist and Ministry*, Faith and Order Paper no. 111, WCC 1982, pp. 20–32 [*BEM*].
[2] *BEM* p. 23.
[3] ARCIC, op. cit., 13.
[4] In Chapter VI above.
[5] *BEM* pp. 21–2.
[6] R. C. Moberly, *Ministerial Priesthood* (1897, reprinted SPCK 1969), pp. 241–2.
[7] ARCIC, op. cit., 13.
[8] *BEM* p. 22.
[9] R. P. C. Hanson, *Christian Priesthood Examined* (Lutterworth 1979), p. 102.
[10] A. M. Ramsey, *The Christian Priest Today* (SPCK 1972), pp. 9–10.
[11] M. Ranken, 'A Theology For the Priest at Work', *Theology*, vol. LXXXV, March 1982, p. 113.

VIII   THE MINISTRY OF PRAYER

It has been stressed more than once that the non-stipendiary minister exercising his ministry at his place of work needs to develop a strong and effective life of prayer, involving a 'holding' ministry of intercession. In a striking essay Martin Thornton draws upon the rich spiritual tradition of the Church to suggest that an appropriate form of this ministry of prayer might be a 'contemplative harmony of place'.

In the seemingly unending search for a suitable adjective to qualify the growing phenomenon – non-stipendiary, auxiliary, supplementary – ministry, I have come to prefer the simple, if still unideal term, amateur. Unideal, since anything from a burglary to a water colour so described implies the incompetent and second-rate; an attitude which in this context I would avoid at all costs. The better connotation is that the amateur is one who plays the game for love not money, and who may well possess a charismatic flair that evades the dour professional. More pertinent to the following considerations, the amateur usually plays for and stays with his home team, without touting his talents around to the highest bidder. He has an inbuilt loyalty to his town or county which he truly represents: amateur Devonians play for Devon.

Amateur clergy embrace a wide range of men, with significant variation in age, occupation, background and abilities. But, to introduce a necessary generalisation, two interrelated characteristics are fairly common to the majority: they are indigenous to an environment and/or comparatively stable. At least there is no professional ladder to climb, no career structure to follow or hope for, for whatever good or bad reason. They are amateurs playing for the home team, whether situated in town, village, school, office or factory. In spite of a mobility affecting all aspects of modern life an amateur priest may well outlast half a dozen stipendiary incumbents and a couple of brace of rural deans.

This characteristic of amateur priesthood is too often treated in terms of expediency bordering on the trivial: these amateurs would be more useful if only they could be shunted around to where they are most needed. And the newly appointed incumbent feels threatened by a popular assistant who has been around the place for a long time. So what are the positive values of this indigenous-stability characteristic?

On the practical level we are dealing with a specific vocation to be a specialist second-in-command, which, if recognised, overcomes the nonsense just mentioned. By analogy the stable amateur is something like the permanent under-secretary in a department of state. He is not the minister in charge, who is liable to flit about from one department to another following a prime minister's reshuffles, but the solid heart of the department, about which he understands more than a dozen ministers put together. The minister is responsible, he is the boss, but heaven help him if he does not listen to his under-secretary with humble seriousness. All of which illuminates the proper relation between stipendiary priest-minister and his amateur colleague. The much more important question is how does this indigenous-stability express itself in terms of spiritual theology?

Ultimately we are dealing with the ascetical implication of the doctrine of creation, which may best be introduced by a very brief historical survey. Both apophatic (renunciative) and kataphatic (affirmative) traditions are rooted in the New Testament, while the former finds its first historical expression within the experiments of the Desert Fathers.

For whatever reasons, and they were various, the Fathers of Egypt fled from the current social and cultural scene; without falling too blatantly into dualistic errors, they reduced material needs to the barest minimum. Food, clothing, houses, cities, were, if not intrinsically evil, at least something of a nuisance to the spiritual quest for God. The tradition became established with the mystical theology of the Pseudo-Dionysius around AD 500 and has continued as a main stream of tradition ever since.

St Benedict quite changed the emphasis – not, as is sometimes suggested, by pandering to human weakness with an attitude of discretion and moderation but by taking the doctrine of creation seriously. Everything human is sanctified by the Incarnation, the whole of human life is bound up with creation, including the body and its appetites. So material things, food, clothing, lands, buildings, are seen not as nuisances to be tolerated but positive vehicles for the divine disclosure, foci for contemplative prayer. In a frequently quoted passage E. L. Mascall puts it well: 'No philosophy of human

67

life can be adequate if it concentrates simply on the relationship in which the individual stands to other human individuals and ignores that in which he stands to the entire universe.'[1] Quite simply, appreciation of the colour scheme of the house and the design of the wallpaper has a lot to do with loving relationships within the family.

And so *stabilitas*: stability within the monastery elevated to the stature of a fourth avowed counsel of Benedictinism. Conversely, mobility, the itchy feet syndrome so prevalent in modern society, not least among younger incumbents, can be a positive hindrance to spiritual development and so to pastoral proficiency. The desire to uproot the amateur-priest-farmer from his farm, or the retired amateur from his solidly based family home, in order that they might fill in a gap elsewhere, is to trivialise vocation and to substitute superficial empiricism for creative ascetical theology.

If the apophatic tradition denies any spiritual significance to the created environment – and this must be respected – St Benedict goes in the opposite direction. *Stabilitas* is no punishment or sanction – he was not dealing with unruly undergraduates confined to bounds, but with dedicated monks whose first steps on the ladder to God were recognition of the presence of God within his creation, exemplified by a contemplative love for creation extended to their environment: fields, gardens, buildings, kitchen, refectory (where you ate and drank), dormitory (where you slept in contemplative comfort), and lavatory (where you washed the body in preparation for the worship of God).

The monastery at Monte Cassino was properly magnificent, not for human comfort, but for the glory of God, and as focus to approaching God, manifested in the flesh. In fine, the monastery, which in later feudal society was not so very different from a secular manor controlled by a Christian lord, was a social community firmly based on an environment which was to be contemplatively loved. Dom Cuthbert Butler puts it like this: 'It may all be summed up in saying that, while for the friar or regular clerk detachment from any particular place is the ideal, in the monk attachment to his own one monastery is a virtue'.[2]

Benedictine *stabilitas* decreed that the abbot of any monastic community be appointed democratically, but thereafter it was for life. Country parsons used to adopt the same outlook, and for similar reasons: fathers of families do not normally change, and when they do it is most unfortunate for all concerned. There follows the domestic, as against the military, emphasis which is characteristic of Benedictinism: families love their homes, they are in contemplative harmony with them in a way that soldiers can hardly love and be in harmony with their barracks.

These Benedictine characteristics – stability, leading to a contemplative rapport with a total environment, including its population, love for creation and domesticity – are repeated throughout Christian history. They are especially pertinent to the Anglican tradition. St Gilbert of Sempringham created a mixed order, very much a family affair, which was indigenous to a restricted area of the English midlands and never departed further afield. Five centuries later the Ferrar family community at Little Gidding arose with adaptable Gilbertine characteristics. All the while from the ninth to the nineteenth century, the English parish was coexistent with a close knit rural community, first the manor then the village, both stable and domestic. The English parochial system is itself of kataphatic, not merely administrative, significance, since it avoids the error which has already been pointed out in the quotation from E. L. Mascall. The parish is not a list of names, neither is it a group of people, but a place: a material environment to which people respond. The parish is part of creation from which human beings cannot be dissociated.

Throughout these centuries, moreover, the parish priest was indigenous to this environment; formerly as a manorial freeman farming his glebe, and latterly the son of a local squire ministering within, or not far from, his home county. He might even be the squire himself, like Sabine Baring-Gould at Lew Trenchard. Failing such immediate environmental rapport the country parson would be presented with a benefice, if at all, at a comparatively early age and remain there for the rest of his life.

If the doctrine of creation is our starting point, then how does this contemplative harmony with God through creation become translated into ascetical theology? J. M. E. McTaggart defined religion, in general, as 'an emotion resting on a conviction of a harmony between ourselves and the universe at large'.[3] E. L. Mascall baptizes this generality by linking it with our incorporation through baptism with the Incarnate Lord who is himself one with creation. In the theology of St Irenaeus Christ is the recapitulation and focus of the whole created universe, and to be recollected in Christ is to be in harmony with the universe.

But how can we make practical sense of the universe in terms of prayer? The traditional answer is by seeing a local environment – parish, school, or factory – as microcosmic of that universe, and finally by seeing some creature, some single thing, as microcosmic of the universe. The most famous example is probably Julian of Norwich and her hazel nut which is 'all that is made ... for God made it, God loveth it, God keepeth it'.[4] Even more practical is Hugh of St Victor's developed method of prayer, based upon the contemplation of creation focused upon a single symbol, a thing, consummated by Christ as perfect and ultimate symbol. It is the mandala technique which, while associated with oriental religion, has been a constant factor in Christian prayer through the crucifix, statue and icon. And it is associated with the concept of the cosmic Christ which, in one form or another, has been around from Colossians to Teilhard de Chardin. Christ recapitulates, absorbs or sums up, the whole universe within himself on the cross because he was intimately united with a little bit of it, namely this small planet inhabited by the human race. Partaking of the high priesthood of the incarnate Lord, the priest contemplatively unites with the parish – environment plus community – and so offers it to the Father, especially as focused in the eucharist.

It is frequently said that one of the main functions of priesthood, especially in its amateur form, is simply being there, recollectively, sacrificially and through intercession. This means much more than being available for consultation and care. Being there is no comfortable theory; it is more than hanging around in case someone needs you. You have to work at it through contemplative prayer, invariably of the mandala type, or according to the Hugh of St Victor technique. No doubt Sabine Baring-Gould prayed for the needs of those who happened to live in Lew Trenchard, but there is a sense in which he did not really have to. A recollective stroll through his beloved little village would have achieved the same thing; it would have been intercessory for the whole environment and everyone who lived in it.

The amateur priest ideally achieves the same effect in parish, school or factory. He may be available in terms of specific pastoral counsel, or in particular intercession, but he does not have to evangelise all through the tea breaks and lunch hours. Recollectively, his work itself can achieve a rapport, a contemplative union with the whole complex, both material and human; but he has to work at it, and initial concentration on the physical environment may be the best way. Back to Mascall!

Hugh of St Victor, Julian of Norwich, St Thomas Aquinas, St Francis and all the saints within this school, concentrate on the symbolism of nature, on trees, birds, flowers and sister louse, but there is no reason why the contemplation of a cog-wheel should not achieve the same thing. What is the modern mandala, the industrial icon? Possibly the school badge, the firm's trade mark or the bank's logo?

If this sounds too deep and complicated, and the application of ascetical theology tends to be simpler in practice than it appears to be in print, the kataphatic saints and teachers are really only pointing to, and adapting in the light of the incarnation, a comparatively common experience. Football teams tend to do better 'at home' than 'away', and I think this is something deeper than being cheered on by the home supporters: the players are more subtly at home within a familiar environment, and there is a rapport leading to a sense of representation and responsibility. But there are differences between amateur and professional. To swop games, the indigenous amateur cricketer, playing for his native county on a ground that he has known and loved since childhood, has a different outlook from the professional, newly signed on from another county for better pay or prospects. Mr Chips loves the school, the whole school and nothing but the school, because it is far more than the staff and the boys. Even a drink in the local tastes a bit different from the same drink in the buffet of a railway station: it is good to be 'at home'.

Closer to context, those concerned with pastoral reorganisation know how difficult it is to persuade well-established parishioners to forsake their parish church for another just down the road. It could be blind prejudice, ultra-conservatism or just plain cussedness; or it could be something very different indeed. It might be an uprooting from a contemplative environment which is creative and intercessory in a deep sense which is difficult to achieve in new surroundings. It is good to be 'at home'.

To be 'at home' is a phrase of such significance that the fourteenth century English asceticists culled the word 'homely' from Middle English and turned it into a subtly technical term, meaning not so much simple or comfortable or unsophisticated as something nearer to contemplatively recollected. Margery Kempe enjoyed 'homely dalliance with the Lord'. In this sense it implies healthy integration, the precise opposite of St Augustine's concupiscence; a contemplative harmony, almost a participation in the love of God for his creation, which is the biblical meaning of his sabbath rest. It is that activity of God which, according to John Macquarrie's interpretation of creation, we now experience as providence.[5]

Can such a creative contemplative state be achieved? The kataphatic saints say it can, and they point the way by theology, method and technique. But to be indigenous to an environment, homely as a native, and domestically or professionally stable, makes it all a good deal easier. The miners, not so unlike the aforementioned established parishioners, object to being removed from their native village to a more productive pit somewhere else. The Coal Board will accuse them of trades union cussedness, and they might be right. Or they might not. If the redundant mining village had produced its indigenous amateur priest it would be well on the way to becoming a spiritually creative organism: in fact, the redemptive Body of Christ. Remove it all to another environment and all is lost. Import an excellent young stipendiary priest from Suffolk and we are back to square one, with twenty years of contemplation-in-place prayer before he can get going. Remove him after five years for preferment to a 'better' parish and we are back to square minus-one. Back to E. L. Mascall, not to mention Julian of Norwich, Hugh of St Victor, St Irenaeus, Aquinas and a good few others! You simply cannot minister to people in a vacuum because people are indissociable from creation.

Of course there are counter-productive snags. Not all amateur priests, however indigenous to an environment, are of kataphatic *attrait*. They may be very holy men of apophatic tendency, feeling that their vocation is best fulfilled by standing well apart from mundane matters and living the priestly life in isolation. They must be encouraged to do it their way.

The indigenous aspect also has its own particular dangers, foremost of which is to confuse tradition with custom. Born and bred in an isolated community, which could be a rural village, a mining community, a slum or a university college, it is all too easy to take custom as sacrosanct and for granted. Liturgy is the obvious case in point: we have always done it this way so we always must. Tradition, on the other hand, is something that moves, that evolves, develops, changes and grows.

If personalities permit, and relations are properly understood, here is the most creative rapport between the the indigenous amateur priest and his stipendiary superior (like 'Father Superior', the man in

72

charge, not 'superior' in the sense of better). The indigenous amateur could support the new incumbent with true wisdom in an environmental situation, with the sort of prayer that the new priest is, in the nature of the case and for no fault of his own, unable all of a sudden to achieve. The imported vicar has the possibility of a clearer vision into the real needs of a community, the most glaring of which can be missed by over-familiarity with custom. The old parson-squire was not too good at necessary innovation. Returning to our former analogy it is the minister of state who has the authority, who must make the decisions, and who should have the insight to make them worthily. The permanent under-secretary may be too enamoured of the policies of former days, yet his stability and experience is of inestimable value.

From the viewpoint herein discussed, subsidiary questions arise, especially concerning selection and training. The Church properly insists that amateur priesthood must not involve any lowering of standards, certainly no double standard implying that the amateur is somehow second-rate. Yet there is an obsession with uniformity which fails to recognise that the amateur may require not inferior but different qualities. Does one who is vocationally attracted to the position of permanent second-in-command need the much-vaunted quality of 'leadership'? Might loyal integrity prove more valuable? Does he need the general qualities of adaptability required by his incumbent or should he rather be a specialist within a team?

The amateur's training raises similar queries. It is the stipendiary priest who by force of circumstances is forced into the administrative jack-of-all-trades role, while the amateur – teacher, doctor, social worker – begins with the bare bones of a built in specialism. Should this not be developed from the start?

But the heart of all priesthood, all ministry, is prayer. It is a Godward calling. No doubt the amateur will teach, preach, and share in the chores, but the core of his ministry is the priestly presence within an environment, a contemplative harmony. And priestly presence, seen as intercessory and redemptive, is more than a comfortable theory. It has to be developed, worked at, prayed into. Amateurs with another job are pressed for time, and they have to find time not in terms of a few evenings for parochial activity, but for daily hours of serious prayer. That is their primary purpose. To be the priestly presence is subtly different from doing the ministerial job.

[1] E. L. Mascall, *The Christian Universe* (Darton, Longman & Todd 1966), p. 91.
[2] C. Butler, *Benedictine Monachism* (Longman, Green & Co. 1924), p. 201.
[3] J. M. E. McTaggart, *Some Dogmas of Religion* (1930), p. 3.
[4] Julian of Norwich, *Revelations of Divine Love,* ed. C. Walters (Penguin 1966), Preface 1.
[5] J. Macquarrie, *Principles of Christian Theology* (SCM Press 1966), pp. 219–24.

IX HOLDING ON

The Church's recognition that the lives of men and women are likely to be shaped as much by communities of work as by communities of place has found expression in a variety of forms of mission and ministry. For example, school chaplains, hospital chaplains, prison chaplains and the like have long held an established position among the ordained ministry. More recently, there have been the industrial chaplains.[1] Their strength, it has been suggested, lies in the fact that they are employed by the Church rather than by the company, or companies, in which they work, and that, because they are not locked into the structure of the company's hierarchy, they can cross the boundaries of management and unions, blue-collar and white-collar workers. and make a more disinterested, and sometimes more perceptive, contribution to the problems which are causing confusion and conflict. Thus the industrial chaplain may exercise a ministry of judgement, mediation and reconciliation, questioning people's assumptions and helping them discover alternative and more fruitful courses of action. His independence is not to be confused with 'neutrality': it gives him room to hear and to be heard. If 'prophecy' is the business of discovering the mind of God in a particular situation, then his ministry may be as much prophetic as it is pastoral.

Industrial chaplaincy is a different form of ministry to the community of work from that of the worker-priest. The latter has a special vocation to exercise his priesthood in a full-time industrial job – often involving manual work of some kind – and to embrace as a priest all the circumstances, stresses, joys and sorrows that go with it. In 1983 the Shop Floor Association, consisting both of priests and of lay persons, revised the terms of its basis as follows:

> *In a world divided between rich and poor we believe that the Gospel must be seen in the first instance as good news for the poor, and in the light of this as good news for society as a whole. Where Christianity is dominated by a middle-class culture this perspective is easily lost. We have chosen to work on the shop floor because it is here that the Gospel calls us, and because it is only from this base that the change we hope for will come.*

One of the members of the Association has written of the role of the worker-priest in the following way:[2]

> *The main theological element of our worker-priest role is the respect for areas of life,*

75

which are not usually considered to be within the influence of the Church, and a recognition of the essential elements within them.

Firstly, a respect for people, who have gained little from our educational system, and are in routine manual and clerical jobs with little interest, skills or responsibility; with this goes a recognition of the practical pressures of life for lower income families in the communities and social groups with the highest level of unemployment.

Secondly, a respect for trade unions, for people's rights to organise, their right to deal with the representative of organised management, and the recognition of what is involved in relationships within trade unions (particularly between members and elected shop stewards and officers), within organised management (particularly between the layers of management), and between the two.

Thirdly, a respect for democracy and political organisation within it and a recognition of what goes on in political parties, between parties, and between parties and the officers of local and national government.

Fourthly, a respect for those facing difficult and controversial issues, which may lead to conflict and where conflict may be an essential part of the route to a solution.

Fifthly, a respect for the role of the lay Christian, facing all these issues day in and day out.

A similar concern for the Church's mission and ministry in the community of work, but taking a very different form, is expressed by Mike Hatt, an NSM whose secular work is that of a Local Authority Engineer. In his job he sometimes finds himself overriding the interests of the individual in favour of what he believes to be the interests of the wider community. He represents the 'powerful' rather than the 'weak'. In his own words, he finds himself 'on the wrong side of the fence'. Yet it is in this sort of situation that he has tried to discover the proper character of his ministry. His reflections are quoted at length, not because his form of ministry at work is any more (or less) authoritative than that of the industrial chaplain or the worker-priest, but because it opens up yet another perspective on the many-sided nature of such ministry. Its emphasis may be pastoral rather than prophetic, but in one more way it expresses the same fundamental concern which characterises the whole of the Church's ministry, whether pastoral, priestly, evangelistic or prophetic, namely that witness should be done in the centre and at the boundaries of human life to the presence and power of God to hold and to heal when things threaten to fall apart.

In Tension

It was a Sunday afternoon and they were glad to see me. I was allowed to hold that precious bundle, their first baby, and although I wasn't wearing my dog collar at the time, it must have looked like any normal parish visit. He was an experienced and hard-working engineer who had worked for me for some while and I had come to tell him that he would be receiving a letter the next day to say 'Your employment is no longer required. I am therefore writing to inform you that you will cease on —— on the grounds of redundancy.' We had been talking about it for some while, but it had been necessary to sacrifice his job in the latest round of staff cuts and he had eventually agreed to go voluntarily to look for a job elsewhere. Those who see the pastoral role of the ministry in dealing with the results of such situations may wish to consider that of the man who initiates redundancies and sees them through to the farewell presentation. It raises particular issues if that man is a priest.

There is a sense in which the individual should expect the priest in the situation to look after his personal interest and join in the struggle against those who oppress him. Society, on the other hand, often sets aside the interests of the individual for the benefit of a wider community, and expects those who work for it to fulfil these expectations. The tensions to which this gives rise are keenly felt by those involved, who may, with all sincerity, be faced with irreconcilable conflicts. There is in this the stuff of the Christian ministry, reconciliation and prayer. There is a need for the conscious presence of the Church of Christ, if only in the symbolic presence of the priest.

We all know the problems of unemployment and the difficulties people have in facing possible redundancy. It is clearly a matter for considerable pastoral concern if a member of one's congregation is threatened with redundancy, particularly if the likelihood of his finding future employment is low. Much pastoral effort has been exercised in recent years over such issues. I would like to look at the other side of the coin, as someone who is involved in the process of making people redundant. As part of a management team, I am necessarily involved and have to deal with these issues with my own staff where someone's job has disappeared, and the opportunities for redeployment seem very low. Am I, I ask myself, involved in a Christian duty? Someone has to do it, but does it have to be me? Certainly I would wish otherwise. Well, I can scarcely deny that I am involved in a pastoral situation. More important, perhaps, my colleagues, also faced with these problems, need support, reinforcement and encouragement in a situation which is to them equally difficult. In a sense I find myself on the wrong side of the fence. In a sense those gathered on that wrong side need to find that the Church

77

is willing to be there too, because if not, what does this have to say about the task they are personally involved in!

I can understand those who dismiss the world of work as wholly secular and point to its many evils, but as long as I belong to a society that not only participates in these processes but also profits by them, I feel a sense of duty, a calling, to be amongst the workers in what they are doing. It would be hypocritical to stand back. Of course, in practice, the world of work is populated by many deeply sincere and in their own way God-fearing people, of whom many are the 'practising Christians' we meet on Sundays. This tension that exists in the practical arena of life, where one person's good may be to another's disadvantage, where success is so often a symbol of exploitation, where caring for one group may lead to the neglect of another – this tension is the creative stuff of prayer in which the priest in the workplace is privileged to participate. The power of such prayer is not to be underestimated, although rarely identified as such. More obvious situations within the workplace do, however, reveal these undercurrents. I have, for example, scarcely ever felt so moved as I did recently at the prayerful support within the office for a colleague and his family when it became known that his wife had just a few months to live. It was not just an expression of concern, or a sense of caring, but more a prayerful working out in the daily lives of all those in that busy office of those feelings both positive and negative that this situation awoke. Her funeral was triumphant.

This dilemma that is represented by the 'good' versus the 'bad' syndrome often places me and me fellow engineers in the position of the 'bad guy'. We are the faceless planners, hell-bent on the destruction of the environment, trampling over the freedoms of the individual. It seems sometimes as if we are thought to shrug off our humanity before we step through the office door in the morning – only to don it again as we go home at night to mow the lawn like normal people. This Jekyll and Hyde perception can bite deep into people who genuinely see themselves fulfilling a valuable role in the service of the public; yet it can be reinforced by the Church's more obvious relationship with the man, or woman, back at home mowing the lawn, rather than with the engineer chopping down trees, or demolishing houses to build more Motorway. As a Civil Engineer engaged in the planning of roads, I find myself involved in Public Consultations or Public Inquiries on road proposals. It is not unusual, and in fact it is to be looked for, that the local church, perhaps its minister, will be involved in supporting those who strongly resist the impact of a major highway on their immediate surroundings. Many a road proposal will require the demolition of people's houses, have an inevitable impact on the environment in the area in which they live and the countryside which they appreciate. The engineer inevitably, therefore, attracts a great deal of hostility from the local community. People have walked up and down the street with banners saying 'Down with Mr Hatt', and at Public Inquiries my pronouncements have been greeted with universal groans. Yet my task is to balance the needs of the community: the need for transport, the need for safety and relief of congestion with the cost of providing relief in terms of money, impact on people and the environment. This balancing act is done with sincerity, and yet to hear the criticisms made one would often doubt it. It is healthy for me to be under such pressure to appreciate the concerns of society. If I look at my colleagues, rewarded in their work by a mountain of criticism, I am glad to be alongside them and to be identified with them in his process. There are many jobs whose rewards are similar in terms of abuse, and yet where a sense of commitment and service to society is important to sustain. Where, I ask myself, should the Church be present?

This dilemma is clearly felt in the workplace. I was intrigued recently when, not long after I had presented a paper to a gathering of fellow professional engineers on the economic benefits and assessment of priorities of highway improvement schemes, one of my staff felt moved to write a poem. When valuing a particular scheme its cost is justified in comparison to the savings made by reducing journey times, saving petrol and, more especially, reducing accidents. It is reckoned, for example, that an 'injury accident' costs society about £4,000, including an allowance for suffering. A human life is valued much higher, at around £150,000. I quote John Richardson-Dawes' poem below with his permission because it points up this tension nicely. It was originally published in our local Trade Union magazine.

Plaintive Cry of a Poet and Traffic Engineer

My worn mind sees its dreams removed, at least what few remained
Of railway romance, English beer and Betjeman,
To where mere costs and benefits count, in physical laws contained
To road design, transition curves and bitumen.

These simulations, exponentials, logarithmic graphs,

Computer programs and speed/flow equations,
Seem to omit some pure essential from within the charts,
And hence my pain, my spiritual abrasions.

If I produced a formula, I might well be believed,
Some highway priest might take up my objections,
Instead they cite the normal distribution, as perceived
By those who've never shared in my reflections.

Oh, shall I leave the traffic flow to infinitely queue
And cast aside the negative binomial?
My probability function can fall to zero now:
An engineer's poetic testimonial.

How then are we to visualise a 'highway priest', this local government officer who is an ordained minister? Assume for a moment that there is such a thing as a typical Christian layman, and imagine asking him or her what they would see as the task of an ordained minister. My expectation is that the response evoked would talk predominantly of those things which happen in, or are associated with, church buildings, and in particular with services of worship. There would be an expectation that certain pastoral commitments would be fulfilled, mainly in terms of visiting, and perhaps Youth Clubs, Mothers' Unions, and similar meetings. This image is perhaps rather a stereotype, but I would anticipate that our 'typical layman' would in fact view Christian ministers very much in stereotype terms.

Now consider the non-stipendiary minister. If the stereotype we have just considered does not really reflect his role in the Church, then the expression 'minister' or 'priest' is difficult to attribute with an understanding of what it means. It is, however, coupled with the negative expression 'not paid', and combines to give a fairly complete picture of uncertainty. This, surprisingly in my view, is one of the great strengths of non-stipendiary ministry, as it has emerged in the Church of England. The uncertainty is evocative of exploration, variety and perhaps adaptation to circumstances. I would always wish to discuss my understandings of non-stipendiary ministry in the context of a wide, uncertain and varied picture. It is an incarnate ministry reflecting the culture within which it lives. It is a varied ministry within the body of Christ, as varied as the many limbs of that body.

Seeking to describe such a form of ministry in terms of traditional ministry is often dangerously like trying to put new wine into old bottles. A number of those who have considered non-stipendiary ministry have noted some uncertainties amongst those who are NSMs. Such uncertainty might well reflect the exploratory nature of the NSM's task at this time, but often I suspect it arises from attempts to make comparisons with traditional ministry roles. My confidence in understanding my own task has developed from setting aside attempts to explain it in those terms. Non-stipendiary ministry, from my viewpoint, is a complementary ministry to that of the traditional parochial ministry. I do not find myself involved in an alternative but rather an additional ministry, with a character quite different in many ways from that of the paid parochial minister.

Society is, of course, no longer organised into tight communities rarely moving beyond their parish boundaries, having the majority of their active lives contained within fairly narrow confines of human relationships. Rather, most of us find ourselves part of a number of different communities or social groupings, of which only one is centred at the place where we live. Sometimes that is one of the least significant of the groups that we are part of, many people these days scarcely knowing the people who live around them. Important groups include the people with whom we work, those with whom we have our social and recreational activities, at sports clubs, the pub down the road, even at the school where our children go, or perhaps attend Scouts, fellow members of professional organisations. These overlapping community groups are the areas in which we exercise our lives as social beings. Much of the debate about deployment of the ministry is in terms of parochial organisation. This is unsurprising. There is, however, some recognition that parochial structures require some development and flexibility.

John Tiller, in his *Strategy for the Church's Ministry,* talks in terms of the local Church being the body of Christ in a particular place and being responsible for undertaking the ministry of the Gospel in its own area. His view of the local Church, although broadening the parochial structure and looking to the deanery as a significant means of co-ordinating the mission of the Church, nevertheless still considers structures in terms of areas and places, rather than of social groupings, such as the local Chamber of Trade, the Bus Company or Trade Union. These are the 'places' where people meet and live out important parts of their lives together. They are places where they express their concerns both in words and action, but they are transient places, formed only by the coincidence of people meeting, rather than any particular geographical location. Amongst such groups there is

81

unlikely to be much consciousness of which parish they meet in, let alone which deanery. Yet if we set aside these groups and suggest that they are doing something quite separate from those areas of life which interest the Church, we are implying that the simple social activities organised by the local Church, which are valuable in their own way, are in some sense qualitatively different from those activities that are 'out of range'. As society has become increasingly mobile (and car ownership has trebled over the last thirty years) so much of our activity has moved away from the places where we live to other areas where we probably feel no particular local loyalty other than to the people with whom we mix.

It is within these areas that the NSM can find himself a natural and welcome part. His task is not, in my view, to abstract from these groups recruits to join his church, either in the form of the building with which he is associated, or in some special little group within the whole, set aside for Christian activity. These are opportunities that already exist in society. The NSM, through his full and genuine involvement in those areas of society of which he is a part, seeks to reveal the presence of the Spirit of God moving throughout his creation, to validate the activity of the Spirit within the ordinary sharing and loving of everyday life, to suffer amongst the failures, disappointments and pain of day-to-day existence, to express the possibility of reconciliation and renewal. The NSM cannot adopt that privileged position of standing outside situations and pronouncing on what is good or bad within them. I am grateful for the fact that I have to live daily in a situation of human frailty, even though often enough the task that I seek to do, as an act of service to society, believing that I do it for the benefit of my fellow men, is regarded as destructive rather than creative.

In the sense that the death of Christ and his resurrection were the culmination of his ministry here on earth, that ministry was in practice a product of his interaction with mankind. It grew out of his involvement in the world. The uniquely Christian incarnate theology exemplifies ministry in a form of service that reacts to man's situation, mediates and redeems. The Church, if it is to be true to Christ, must bear the marks of a true engagement with the world, however difficult or painful a process that may be. That is not to say, of course, that the ministry of Christ as observed was one of continuous pain and suffering – far from it. There were moments of great joy and sharing in happiness and love alongside the disappointments and frustrations.

82

As the hymn says, God is working his purpose out, and so the Christian understanding of the Creator at work is of a continuous process of salvation and mediation. In so far as the Church is involved in working out the purpose of God, so its ministry will reflect these attributes. However, just as Christ exercised his ministry in time and place, so our ministry reflects the variety and ranges of times and places in which we all individually live. The process of mediation reflects the situation to which it is addressed.

I have to say that after fifteen years as a 'minister in secular employment' I have come to appreciate the processes of creative tension with which I live. At times the tension is expressed in prayer, not just praying on one's feet but more likely at the gallop, and yet with those brief flashes of eternity that allow everything to be said. On other occasions it is a conflict of ideologies biting deep into one's consciousness, challenging all that is being struggled for, bringing man in his hopelessness face to face with his undying need for God. Sometimes it is a sadness that the very glory of God being worked out in the lives around me goes unseen. More often it is a search for a valid Christian existence in a part of the world from which the visible Church and its ways seem to have withdrawn. And if as the years move on I find in my own experience some signs of hope, some authentication of the action of the Spirit of God out there in his creation, some valid Christian response, then with others so moved I can, as a priest within that situation, be a sign of that validity. At least that is how it seems to me as I choose – indeed believe I am truly called – to live in the tension of ordination to the priesthood.

---

[1] In what follows we draw upon some reflections by the Rev. Alan Christmas, Industrial Chaplain to the Bishop of Oxford.

[2] We are grateful to the Rev. Tony Williamson, who works on the shop floor at the BL factory at Cowley, for contributing these reflections.

X TAKING STOCK

Whether an ordained minister of the Church is paid a stipend by the Church for the ministry he exercises on its behalf, or whether his ministerial work is voluntary and unpaid, would not in itself appear to be a matter of grave theological significance. There is no obvious theological or ethical principle requiring either that he should be paid or that he should not be paid. On the one hand the labourer is worthy of his hire. On the other hand, he may wish to give his service as a free-will offering.

Questions may begin to arise, however, when a contrast is drawn between 'full-time' and 'part-time' ministers. The problem does not obtrude itself so much if one is thinking simply in functional or job categories. Part-time jobs are just as respectable, though not as remunerative, as full-time jobs. Moreover, even the 'full-time' minister ought to have 'time off', for example for recreation or to spend with his family. Ordained ministry ought not to be a seven days a week and twenty-four hours a day job, even though the nature of the job is such that in certain circumstances it is difficult not to be 'on call'. However, ordination cannot adequately be encompassed in functional categories. There is a sense in which it is as odd to speak of a part-time ordained minister as it would be to speak of a part-time baptized Christian. There are various ways of spelling out this more-than-functional aspect of ordination. They involve different philosophical concepts. For example, one might speak of the 'character', or 'stamp', given by ordination. Or one could point to its 'ontological' significance apart from the specific functions which an ordained minister is authorised to fulfil. Let us begin by saying that what an ordained minister is is as important as what he does, even though, of course, being and act cannot be totally separated from each other. And what a person is by virtue of his ordination, might be further described, in yet another philosophical conceptuality, in symbolic terms. As an ordained minister he becomes a special symbol within the total Christian symbolic system. He is, one might wish to say, a representative symbol, representative of Christ in his Church and representative of the Church in Christ. Or, combining philosophical with theological language, one might describe him as a sacramental symbol. (Symbols, it should be noted, are not external and arbitrary signs of that which they symbolise; rather, they participate in the reality which they symbolise. The 'symbolic' world must not be set over against the 'real' world, as if it were only a pale shadow of it, itself 'unreal' and ultimately dispensable. Some realities can be communicated only through the use of a rich symbolism. In these cases the real and the symbolic cannot be prised apart. In this sense, then, the reality of God's self-communication to his creatures is itself a symbolic reality.)

Through ordination a minister is given a special place in the Christian symbolic reality. Such a way of putting things is a more reflective expression of the unreflective idea that the ordained minister is 'set apart'. He is now associated with the world of the 'holy' and has to deal with 'holy' things. As James Mark has stressed,[1] it is by his power and authority to handle holy things that the priest is characteristically differentiated from other ministers of the Church. After noting the priest's role as guardian of the tradition, and therefore as pastor and public spokesman, he refers especially to the ministry of the sacraments, 'since it is the one ministry that the laity may not normally initiate':

It has to do with the Christian mysteries, in a sense that lies beyond and below the use of words: and the role of priesthood is ultimately based on it. We see this in other religions: it was, after all, the distinctive function of the priesthood in the Judaism of the Old Testament. We see it in the correlation between the emphasis that individual Christian denominations place on the sacraments and that which they place on the priesthood, so that the Society of Friends, which has no sacramental ministry, has no separate priesthood. Where there is an emphasis on sacred things there is a corresponding emphasis on responsibility for handling them. And this, in turn, leads to an emphasis on the choice and control of those who themselves control sacramental actions – a choice and control which are expressed in ordination to the priesthood. This is thought to be necessary so that due order and reverence may be ensured. The actual skills involved are not hard to learn, but the actions have to be performed by a limited number of people whom it is, in theory, possible to control. Hence, in the Middle Ages there was the concept of the massing priest who was trained to say the mass and to do little else: but such a notion would be unacceptable nowadays. We expect the person who celebrates to understand in some measure what he is doing and what underlies it. He must therefore also be able to exercise the ministry of the Word. But responsibility for the sacraments remains the peculiar function of the

85

priesthood in most Christian traditions, including the Anglican: that responsibility rests with people set aside for the task: ordained to it, in fact. So long as the Anglican tradition remains rooted in this kind of folk-experience and in the feelings to which it gives rise, the situation is unlikely to change.

In referring to 'folk-experience' James Mark has, I believe, hit upon something extremely important, namely, that there may be a deep-lying tension between Christian and 'folk' concepts of holiness. Christian ideas and institutions do not exist within a kind of spiritual vacuum. They find expression in a given culture which has its own historical traditions and presuppositions, and to a greater or less extent they are subject to the influence of that culture. Thus there arises the possibility, if not the inevitability, of tension, whether creative or destructive, and it is because of this that careful thought needs to be given to anthropological as well as theological considerations. Popular expectations of ministry are as relevant to its exercise as are theological definitions.

It has been pointed out[2] that there is a remarkable tendency in diverse human societies to place their priests and laymen in separate, clearly demarcated categories. The set-apartness of priests is emphasised when candidates are recruited from a limited selection of the population, such as a caste or lineage, as with the Brahman priests of India or the Levitical priests of the Old Testament. They are then further marked out by virtue of their special training and the rite of ordination. They are generally required to adopt distinctive dress, sometimes a tonsure, and clearly defined roles in both religious and social organisations. Their way of life not infrequently requires celibacy and, in Robertson Smith's words, 'ritual observances and precautions too complicated for the layman to master . . . habitual practices of purity and asceticism which cannot be combined with the duties of ordinary life'.

In the Christian tradition a sacerdotal theology of ministry, which intensifies the priest–layman distinction, developed as early as the third century and became elaborated in the Middle Ages, and indeed for most of Christian history the tradition of the Church has in one way or another opted for priests who, in common with the clergy of most other faiths, have been set apart in a category clearly distinguishable from that of the laity.

Underlying this clear demarcation of the priestly and lay categories is the feeling that the world of ordinary everyday life and the world of

86

the holy are two different worlds, each with a power and reality of its own, and that it is not only confusing but also dangerous to remove the boundary lines and allow a free and unregulated association between them. The holy, especially, can be destructive, and therefore has to be handled with the utmost caution and care. It cannot be ignored, but it must be kept in its place and may not be familiarised or treated casually.

Christian theology cannot but be critical of this deep human feeling about the holy. Of course, God is holy and therefore, in a sense, transcendent and totally other. He is not part of our ordinary world, nor is he the world as a whole. Moreover, as God he evokes a sense of creatureliness and even of fear, since it is a fearful thing to fall into the hands of the living God and the fear of the Lord is the beginning of wisdom. God cannot be domesticated. On the other hand, the Christian gospel is the good news of the coming of God to his world, of the Word made flesh, of the transcendent in our midst. God's holiness does not keep him away from the world; therefore the world itself must be capable of receiving holiness. It is ordinary bread that becomes life-giving food, ordinary wine that becomes the medicine of salvation. Thus the secular does not necessarily exclude the holy. On the contrary, the holy can indwell and transfigure the secular. Holiness is essentially a characteristic of God, but by God's grace the created order may participate in the holiness of God.

From the point of view of Christian theology the holy and the secular have to be distinguished, but they are not mutually exclusive. People and things may become holy, not through acquiring some new power of their own, but by being re-established in a right relationship with God. In becoming holy they remain, in a sense, the creatures they were; in another sense, however, they are a new creation.

From a theological point of view, then, the relation between the holy and secular is neither one of identity nor one of contradictory opposition. In so far as the world pretends to self-sufficiency, God stands over against the world. In so far as the world acknowledges its dependence on God, God is for the world and present to the world. Transcendence and immanence both characterise God's relationship to the world, a relationship which because of the faithfulness of God is constant and trustworthy, but which because of the changeableness of the world is at the same time itself dynamic and changing.

Let us call this God–world relationship 'incarnational'. (This may not be the right word for it, but for our purposes it does not matter.)

Then we may call the Christian understanding of holiness incarnational. Furthermore, we may say that the symbolism which is expressed in the person of the ordained priest should itself be incarnational. He should symbolise both the otherness of God – and so the unholiness of the world when claiming an ultimacy and self-sufficiency – and the potential holiness of the world when attentive and obedient to its Creator. He should symbolise both the world-confronting and the world-affirming elements of the Christian understanding of Christ and the Church. How this double witness can best be expressed may vary from age to age, situation to situation, and even individual to individual. The emphasis will vary, now inclining to the one pole, now to the other.

Those who are suspicious of the principle of a non-stipendiary ministry are anxious lest, by being closely involved in the interests, structures and powers which shape the life of the world – whether or not his place of work is seen as the primary place of ministry – the non-stipendiary minister may dangerously weaken the symbolic reference of ordination to the world-confronting aspect of the Christian faith. Those, on the other hand, who favour a non-stipendiary ministry in principle see it as an opportunity to give expression to the world-affirming aspect of the Christian faith. What they are anxious about is the danger that those in the Church may forget, and those outside the Church may never realize, that God's rule extends over the world as well as over the Church.

The ambiguities of life in the world are inherent in that life. They cannot be nicely delimited. There are a few kinds of job and profession which the Church has traditionally considered to be incompatible with Christian discipleship, but it is not only these which occasion concern. It is the fact that the fundamental force of life in the world seems to be the need to survive and the prevailing motive in human affairs seems to be a more or less enlightened self-interest. Neither the need to survive nor the motive of self-interest is in itself necessarily sinful, but they can both very quickly turn into something selfish, destructive and even demonic. On the other hand it is precisely in the midst of these ambiguities that the saving grace of God can reveal itself in judgement, mercy and renewal. The tension between world and Church is creatively sustained in the rule of God.

Within an 'incarnational' theology of the kingdom of God it could well be argued that the exercise of a non-stipendiary ministry, with its symbolic emphasis on the priority of God's 'yes' to the world over his 'no', should be at least as normative as the exercise of a stipendiary ministry. On the other hand, since the Church also has a prophetic ministry of witness 'over against' the world in its pretensions to self-sufficiency, this witness also needs symbolic expression, and it could be argued that it is more clearly expressed in the exercise of a ministry freed from the need to make its own way within the secular structures of the workaday world. Theological considerations, it would appear, embrace both forms of ministry. They are complementary to each other. It is the varied practical aspect of ministry, rather than the underlying theological rationale, which over the course of time has come to favour the exercise of a stipendiary rather than a non-stipendiary ministry. Consequently, if changing practical considerations today suggest the development of a non-stipendiary ministry, they need not be dismissed simply because they are practical, so long as the supporting theology is developed *pari passu*.

There is, as we have seen, a unified and unifying theology of the ordained ministry which permits – indeed encourages – this ministry to be exercised in different forms. These different forms will require the development of different skills, and a move from one form of the ministry into another will no doubt call for the development of new skills. But it is the same ministry which will be exercised. We may call it the ministry of word and sacrament. We may call it the communication of the gospel in word and deed. Different persons will exercise this ministry in different ways, according to personality and circumstance. But by virtue of their ordination they will be representative symbols of Christ in his Church, authorised by the Church to have that symbolic and representative role.

Those who have moved from non-stipendiary to stipendiary ministry, or vice versa, have no doubt had a mixture of motives for making the move. But those who have reflected self-consciously on what they have done and why they have done it have insisted that the change has been occasioned by a change in their personal circumstances rather than a change in their understanding of what ordained ministry is really about. Thus Alan Payne, who was ordained as an NSM, exercising his ministry primarily through his work as a teacher, and then moved to the parochial ministry, has stressed the fact that the fundamental vocation is to ministry, not to some particular exercise of it.

It seems to me that vocation is to ministry i.e. priesthood (which I take to be to do with representation of the body of Christ, the focusing of the

89

calling of Christian), leadership, the exercise of authority in the Church, reconciliation, proclamation of the kingdom. Vocation is to do such things or be such a person (depending on your theological stance), not to be stipendiary or non-stipendiary. It is the mistake of the 'clerical profession' to identify ministry with a particular institutional expression of ministry. Which of the two circumstances of ministry is chosen is a matter of what is appropriate to the person's age, financial and family circumstances, as well as to the Church's financial situation and needs in terms of time commitment etc.[3]

When Alan Payne changed the form of his ministry he did not consider it a change of vocation, the essence of the ordained ministry being an authorised representation of the Church.

The springs of my vocation to a ministry at work were a realisation of the marginal impact of the institutional Church upon the sphere in which I worked, and the invisibility of the lay Christian at work. By the latter I do not mean lack of commitment or effort to put faith into practice. There certainly was considerable ministry of caring, dedication to work and moral concern which individuals would see as arising from and sustained by their faith. This however was mostly a private response and missing from the Christian witness were the elements of prophecy or discernment of spirits, of proclamation of the kingdom, of interpretation of the experience of the work situation in the light of Christianity. My conclusion was that the church needed authorised representation . . .

It seems to me that the non-stipendiary minister who has a work focused ministry, whether or not this includes the celebration of the eucharist, exercises a ministry which is of the essence of ordained ministry as much as the priest who is stipendiary and presides over the parish, indeed he possibly exercises a part of priesthood which, because of increasing sacramentalism in the church and fragmentation and compartmentalising of our lives, has been neglected. I therefore do not see non-stipendiary ministry and stipendiary ministry as radically different nor do I see transfer from the former to the latter, especially where there is a determination to bring the experience of work and ministry at work to the parish situation, as a change of vocation.

In similar manner, Anthony Birbeck, who after seventeen years in the stipendiary ministry, most of them as an industrial chaplain, joined a small company as a management consultant, has expressed the conviction that he has been exercising the same fundamental ministry in both, understood in terms of a theology of the kingdom of God and of a ministry representative of the ministry of the people of God in God's world. This he finds expressed, 'perhaps ironically', in some words of Ruth Etchells about training for the non-professional-ised, non-stipendiary lay ministry.[4]

> To be called to lay service is to be called to live fully in the secular world, to be at ease in it, to know its idioms and its assumptions, because one's centre is there. It is not to sally out from one's 'real' centre, the parish church and its affairs . . . for sorties into industry or trade or education or politics or whatever. It is to live in industry or trade or education or politics, to earn one's income from them (or to be employed by them); to be committed to them; and there, in that place where one's energies are committed, to engage quite consciously in mission and ministry.

What then does he see to be the point of ordination?

> My own experience, the meaning of which in my present role is slowly emerging, suggests that the added value of ordination may be twofold. First, that by the presence of an ordained person in secular employment, those lay men and women who are trying to, or who would like to, see their work as a valid form of mission and ministry are encouraged and supported simply by his presence. Second, that the non-stipendiary minister, if able to find time and energy, can catalyse others in a parish to create a small group for support in and understanding of the world of which they are all part. It may start in very ordinary and, some may say, trivial ways: through the way in which he preaches or leads intercessions and in conversations at odd moments, enriching in a small way the life of the congregation, or of individuals in it, by his own experience and thoughts.
>
> But there are two fundamental prerequisites. The one is to take secular work and its setting absolutely seriously and be proficient there. The other is to have a grounding in theological understanding and the ability to relate fundamental and major Christian themes to what is experienced. I cannot imagine doing what I have done over the years without such a grounding and continuing development of insight and understanding. I have often thought that being a theologian – however humble – has been more important than being ordained in order to exercise ministries in the work setting. I would have found it difficult to have seen my present work as a deliberately chosen form of ministry and mission were it not for such training and development in theological understanding; as it is, there is a sense in which I feel myself to be much more committed to what I believe and stand for than was ever the case as a diocesan priest and canon. I suppose that is the result of the ever-present awareness of being a priest and the need, for my own sake and others', to answer the question, 'Why?'[5]

Non-stipendiary ministry of one sort or another has a long history in the life of the Church. If some of its more recent developments strike one as new, they are nonetheless developments of an existing tradition and not the beginning of a new tradition. Although these developments have been prompted, at least in part, by changing circumstances and practical considerations, there is no *a priori* theological reason why they should immediately be ruled out of court. On the other hand, clear theological criteria need to be established so that these developments may be carefully monitored and wisely directed. What some of these criteria are has, it is hoped, been becoming more transparent in the course of the preceding chapters.

1. There needs to be a robust theology of the kingdom of God, according to which Church and world are both, in their distinct but related ways, recognised as spheres of God's creative and redemptive work, so that one of the functions of the Church is to witness to the fact that the world as much as the Church is dependent upon God. God's 'Yes' and 'No' to the world find an echo in the Church's 'Yes' and 'No' to the world.

2. The ordained ministry of the Church is representative of the ministry of Christ in his Church. As such, it too will reflect both God's 'Yes' and God's 'No' to the world.

3. The ordained ministry of the Church is essentially one and the same, representative, symbolic and sacramental. There are no 'first-class' and 'second-class' priests, no 'full-time' and 'part-time' ministers. It is a communication of the grace of God, a ministry of word and sacrament, implicit and explicit, secular and ecclesial.

4. The ordained ministry of the Church is exercised in different places in different ways. There will therefore be different gifts, different skills and different emphases in training.

5. However and wherever they exercise their ministry, ordained ministers are called and authorised by the Church and need the continuing support of the Church. They 'belong' both to the worshipping community of the Church and also to the community, of place or work, to which they are ministering.

---

[1] In an essay on the theology and work of Readers, published as an occasional paper by the Central Readers' Conference.

[2] For example, in a private letter from Dr Mark Hodge to the editor, from which much of what follows is drawn.

[3] From an essay about the experience of transferring from non-stipendiary to stipendiary ministry.

[4] From an unpublished paper.

[5] From an essay about the experience of transferring from stipendiary to non-stipendiary ministry.